The Thin Line Between Love and Hate

by

Michelle A O'Connor

Bloomington, IN  Milton Keynes, UK

authorHOUSE®

AuthorHouse™
1663 Liberty Drive, Suite 200
Bloomington, IN 47403
www.authorhouse.com
Phone: 1-800-839-8640

AuthorHouse™ UK Ltd.
500 Avebury Boulevard
Central Milton Keynes, MK9 2BE
www.authorhouse.co.uk
Phone: 08001974150

First published by AuthorHouse 11/20/2007
ISBN: 978-1-4259-8871-5 (sc)

Printed in the United States of America
Bloomington, Indiana

This book is printed on acid-free paper.

Library of Congress Control Number: 2006911207

Contents

About the Author   vii

Chapter 1 ❤   1
Miss Cowdidoo's Daughter

Chapter 2 ❤   9
My Escape

Chapter 3 ❤   17
Birth Order

Chapter 4 ❤   23
Boy Meets Girl

Chapter 5 ❤   39
Conflict Resolution

Chapter 6 ❤   45
Love Is a Verb

Chapter 7 ❤   53
Crossing the Line

Chapter 8 ❤   61
The Power of Hate

Chapter 9 ❤   69
True Colors

Chapter 10 ❦   77
We Are More Alike Than We Think

Chapter 11 ❦   83
My Knight in Shining Armor

Chapter 12 ❦   91
I Still Believe in God

Chapter 13 ❦   97
Finally, Brethren

Chapter 14 ❦   103
I Am Truly Grateful

About the Author

As the youngest child in my family, I realized early that I was markedly different from my siblings. When our personalities began to clash, my parents never intervened, and an abusive sibling relationship resulted at a very young age.

Eventually, I had no choice but to stay away from my family. While life was calm for a while, my siblings were bent on destroying me, and they capitalized on every chance they got. I realized then that they genuinely hated me, and I concluded that there really is a thin line between love and hate.

This book chronicles and examines that family life—the life I loved, the life I left, the life that hate destroyed, and the life that love rebuilt. Hate is a dangerous emotion, and many don't realize that love and hate are only separated by a thin line ...

Love begins at home, and it is not how much we do... But how much love we put in that action.

Mother Teresa

Chapter 1 ❦

Miss Cowdidoo's Daughter

I was born the youngest of four children, three girls and a boy, in the small community of Hayes in Clarendon, Jamaica. My sister Grace was the oldest, followed by my brother Rocky, my sister Dawn, then me. While my siblings were born within a four-year time span, I was born nearly five years after Dawn. We lived on nearly two acres of land, just enough for my father to raise his cattle, my mother to do chicken farming, and plenty of room for my goats.

My parents did not have much money, but because my father was a mason and was able to build our house, we were able to live in a comfortable four-bedroom home. Dawn and I shared a room and a queen-sized bed. Rocky's bedroom was a smaller room behind ours. Grace had a large room on the opposite side of the house, and my parents' room was right in front of mine.

My father was the proverbial "tall (more than six feet), dark, and handsome" man. My mother was barely five feet, but a beautiful woman with large breasts—a black Dolly Parton without the voice. All three of my older siblings were almost as tall as my father, but I was a little taller than my mother, a little over five feet. While my sisters wore sizes anywhere from 12 to 16, I wore sizes between 6 and 8. We not only had very different personalities, but we also looked different as well.

We were all members of the Seventh-Day Adventist Church and all held active positions at some time or another. My brother and sisters were all accomplished church singers, but I was different; I was the talker. My mother had once been the church clerk, and my father was a deacon. Even though I did not have a close relationship with my sisters and brother, Dawn, whom I followed in birth order, was caring and protective of me when we were young children. At one point, Rocky and I became close and went to church functions and holiday celebrations in the parish together. During that time, I first took an interest in learning the game of cricket and reading *Time* magazine. Well, actually, Rocky read *Time* and told me what was going on in the world.

When I was very young, I stayed home with my mother while my older siblings went to school. I had little games that I played with her. I used to go to the gate at our house and call my mother by her name pretending to be someone else. When she came out to me, I said, "My mother would like for you to keep me until she gets home." When I wanted something in particular to eat I told her that "Miss Cowdidoo" said that she should cook it for me. Miss Cowdidoo was my imaginary mother. Anything I asked my real mother for, I told her that Miss Cowdidoo said she should do it for me or give it to me until she got back. My brother and sisters began teasing me about having an imaginary mother. When we got into an argument, they told me to "go home to my mother." After I started school and made my own real friends, however, Miss Cowdidoo became a lesser part of my life. I spoke about her less and less to my family and eventually told them that she immigrated to England.

The year I started primary school they changed the school day to the shift system. This is where the wchool population is divided into two, one goes to school at 7am and ends at noon. The other shift begins at noon and end at 5pm. The shift system was a solution to the extemely over crowed problem most school were experiencing.

Unfortunately, Dawn and I ended up in different shifts. My mother tried to move me to Dawn's shift, but the other first grades were overcrowded and could not take me. So, I had to go to school by myself and was often beaten by other children. Afterward, my mother moved me to another school in a different community, and I attended full days of school with my neighbor

Suzie. She was about three years older than I and was very protective of me. Once when I was waiting for her class to finish, one of the older girls approached me, took off her belt, and started to beat me. When I ran to find Suzie, she found the girl, held her down, and let me beat her up. That was so much fun! The following September, Suzie began attending high school, while I was left in the third grade. By this time, though, I was able to defend myself from the bullies and even started a few fights of my own.

Back on the home front, I wasn't feeling very much a part of my family. My siblings, being years older than I was, were not really my playmates. In fact, they didn't play with me at all. I played as much as I could with my friends at school before I was supposed to be home. I also got involved in as many school activities as possible. I was active in both the singing and the speech choirs, which represented the school at festivals and other functions. I also developed a wonderful relationship with my third-grade teacher, Miss Allison, and visited her in her home from time to time. At one point, she even invited me to spend Easter with her, but my mother wouldn't let me go. My life revolved around the institutions of church, school, and home. I tried to have as much fun as I could at church and school since I did not feel a part of the family to which I belonged.

Grace moved to Canada to live with our grandmother, but the relationship between Dawn and Rocky never changed after she left home. Rocky became overly aggressive to me at this time. I remember being in primary school trying to learn multiplication when I was seven years old. Rocky was about fourteen at that time. Most of our school notebooks had multiplication tables in the back, but for some reason, mine only contained metric tables. So I cut the multiplication tables off of the back of Rocky's notebook instead, so I could study my multiplication. When he found out, he slapped me across the face so hard that his fingerprints were left on my cheek. When my mother looked at my cheek, I could see such pain on her face. She took me into the kitchen to sit with her for the rest of the day. This set the precedent for how conflict was resolved in my family. When my siblings hit me, my mother took me away from the situation without ever reprimanding them. The only one I never had much conflict with was Dawn, because she was a very protective big sister to me.

After two years of living in Canada, Grace returned home. Unfortunately for me, she joined right in with my other aggressive siblings and beat me, too. To make matters worse, our father gave them permission to beat me as long as they wanted. They only needed to save the eyes. So they took the beatings to the limit, whether or not they were justified. I remember on one occasion after my father painted our house, and placed the paint brushes in a pan to soak the point out. Grace was sitting beside the brushes. I went to sit beside her, picked up the soaked paintbrush, and proceeded to run the brush across both my foot and hers. She was so angry that she chased me through the house and called Dawn to hold me down so that she could beat me. Dawn asked, "What has she done?"

But Grace only responded with, "Hold her down!" So, for some reason, Dawn obeyed, and Grace beat me for the paint job.

Grace was always beating me for the least little thing. Because the beatings were so severe, I don't always remember all of the details. But I do remember that they always happened over minor incidents, even when the incidents didn't have anything to do with me. One time, my cousin who was living with us told Grace and me that he lost some money. So, for some reason, maybe thinking that I stole the money, Grace beat me with my mother's baking tin. At this point, I knew I had to tell someone, so I told my grandmother, my father's mother. My grandmother went to my father and spoke to him about it. He came and called Grace and me and asked us what happened. It seemed as if he was really concerned, and I just started to cry, and I could not explain to him what happened. I was not used to seeing my parents' concern over the abuse I received from my siblings, so I did not know where to begin.

Church, school, and the two acres of land were my refuge. When I was home, I just tried to avoid everyone by staying in my room and reading. Or I would sit under a tree for a long time just thinking and making sure I stayed out of everyone's way. My friend Suzie started giving me magazines to read, and I started a magazine exchange with my friend Shernett, so I always had plenty of fresh reading material. My magazine collection consisted of *Oh Boy* from Great Britain and *Plain Truth*, which was full of attention-getting true stories. Rocky was still not satisfied that I was staying away from them, so when he saw me reading, he snatched my magazine away from me and asked, "Whatcha reading?" and told me not to read them anymore.

When I was thirteen, I was selected to represent my church at the summer camp Verley at St. Catherine, which was the neighboring parish to Clarendon where I attended church. It was so exciting to be selected to go to the camp meeting and make a report to my youth group when I returned. I was provided a list of items to take with me for eight days, and I was expected to attend different events that required me to change clothes several times per day. By the time I finished packing, I left with one large suitcase, a bag of shoes, and my pillow. My mother asked a family friend to pick me up and take me to my aunt's friend, Yevett, in Spanish Town near Camp Verley. Yevett was going to camp as a staff member, so she took me with her.

Camp Verley was eight days full of fun and lots of activities, such as swimming, hiking, arts and crafts, debate, singing, and games. We had devotions in the mornings, which were organized and led by the campers, and I got a chance to be a part of that. The day before camp ended, we held a banquet, where I had my first date. At the end of the eight days, all of us campers felt as if we had known each other all our lives. We hugged and cried as we exchanged addresses.

The day I was supposed to go home, however, I realized I had a serious problem—I was so excited to get to camp that I didn't bother to figure out how I was going to get home! So I asked Yevett whether she had made arrangements for me to get home. She told me not to worry because she would make plans for me to go home.

She took me to her house, and her friend took care of me, and then she made arrangements for Ken, the family friend my mother had asked to take me to camp, to take me home. Yevett was my hero that day, because even though she had so many responsibilities of being a camp counselor, she still shouldered the burden of asking her friend to take care of me for a few days while she finished up her responsibilities at camp.

After I returned home, I received a good beating from Rocky for not returning home from camp the day it was over. I was expected to take three different methods of transportation all by myself with one suitcase and a bag, at age thirteen years old. If I had gotten off the bus at the last stop, I would have had to walk by myself, because my parents did not make any arrangements for me to reach home, so I thought the best thing to do was to go back home the same way I left.

By the time I was born into the family, my parents were not the ones in charge of my discipline—my sisters and brother were. So, they convinced my parents that I should have come home right after camp. Unfortunately, nobody bothered to question whether that was possible. I was not allowed to defend my point of view—what my siblings said was final. So, after I returned from camp, Rocky took off his belt and gave me a fine piece of beating. I started to feel the pain before he even hit me, not from the belt but from the injustice. Even though he beat me over and over again, I couldn't cry; I just sat there and stared. That absolutely enraged him, and he shouted, "What a wicked little pickny! She won't even cry!" So, he beat me harder, as if he were going to kill me; so, fearing for my life, I had to start crying for him to stop. I am not sure if I ever felt the beating, but I felt the injustice, the shame, and the fact that I was alone in the world.

I was relieved when my youth leader called me one day at church and said he heard about what had happened. After I explained to him exactly what happened, he seemed to understand my side of the story and could not understand the rationale for the beatings. I knew he was confused and disappointed over what was happening in my home, but I felt he had a distinct sense of empathy and sympathy toward me. After that incident, he made an effort to involve me in every church activity. He allowed me to go on summer trips even though I had no money and allowed me to participate in competitions with other churches.

The incident of Rocky beating me had an unimaginable emotional impact because it was wrong on so many levels. It was wrong for my parents to give him the power of discipline. Rocky was only seven years older than me; he was not able to execute the judgment of a parent. Unfortunately, my parents didn't seem to be able to do it either. Afterward, I thought of running away, but the only two places I could go were my aunt's house in Montego Bay and my mother's relatives' home in Portland. I figured, "What's the use? They'll look for me anyhow," so it made no sense to leave. At this point, more than ever, I truly wished that I was Miss Cowdidoo's daughter. I did not want parents who were going to put up with the wrongs done to me.

I was a child and a human; I wasn't perfect. I expected my parents to reprimand me and to tell me what I did wrong, so I knew the right thing to do next time. I expected them to be angry with me when I upset them and let me know they were angry, because they were my parents and I was a child—their child—not the child of my brother and sisters. But I vowed that I was going to make it. I did not have a real mother or a father. I was alone in this world, so I made a vow to take care of myself.

The one thing I needed was an education. Since it was the one thing that my mother tried to give us more than anything else in the world, I finally had something in my favor. After Rocky beat me, I had only one goal—to get an education so that I could earn a living and never have to depend on anyone ever again. As soon as that happened, I would leave home. In the meantime, I did everything I could to avoid being any trouble to anyone. I became the first of the four of us children to open a bank account. My sisters ridiculed me because I opened my account with only $20. But I didn't care, because it was the beginning of my independence. Then I started learning to budget. I saved part of every bit of money I received and deposited it in my account. I was soon able to afford things that my mother could not give me.

After that, I paid my own way to camp, bought my own clothes, and paid for my own school trips. I tried my best in school and participated in many activities. I had fun at school because I had close friends and a good relationship with my teachers. When I came home, I stayed in my room, avoided Rocky and my sisters, and tried to please my parents. By this time, I started believing that my sisters and brother were happy before I was born and all I did was upset their wonderful world.

Fate chooses your relatives you chose your friends.

Chapter 2 🌣

My Escape

At this point, I never really thought that my sisters and brother hated me. I just had a very strong feeling they behaved the way they did simply because I was an intruder. The three of them had already formed a bond before I came along, so they were not willing to share their space with me. So I said, "Fine with me; I'll go find my own people to attach myself to." I was certainly not going to force myself where I wasn't wanted, and the battle of three against one was becoming a little hard to win. So I did the next best thing to forming close family bonds. I realized that outside of my home, I made friends easily and was very well liked. So I tried to establish my personal identity, goals, and aspirations. Then I could find friends who embraced my ideals. That's a very hard job for a teenager, but that's exactly what I did.

Jackie and Judith Peart were two sisters who attended May Pen High School where I was a student. They were focused, disciplined, talented, well mannered, and full of fun. They had a sister named Janet, wonderful parents, and a lovely home for me to escape to. Being friends with the sisters became a big part of my life. I spent many of my weekends and a part of my summer holidays there. I found this family to be a very interesting and welcome change to my own. The girls' mother was quite soft-spoken and never seemed to use harsh discipline, yet the girls behaved so well. And they had such an organized routine in their home life. Mrs. Peart worked at home as a seamstress. She worked six days per week and was well established. She went to her sewing room from 9 a.m. until late afternoon when she would make dinner. The girls made their own clothes, completed their household duties, and fell into their roles without much prompting from their mother.

Mr. Peart was like a silent partner. He got up in the morning, ate his breakfast, and went to work. In the evenings, he came home, ate his dinner, and went to his room. He walked around the yard sometimes but never said much. The sisters also had a brother named Dave who was always in his room. Janet was about two years older than Jackie who was the same age as I was, right down to the month, while Judith was a year younger. What truly fascinated me about the Pearts was that they focused on having a good relationship with each other.

I exchanged letters with Judith and Jackie during the summer months, and sometimes, I'd visit them for a whole day at their house. When we felt that the holiday needed some more fun, we gathered our friends together and went to the beach. Although we did not have much money, we still planned a big event out of what we had. We made a list of the things we needed, figured how much money each person could contribute, and split the list among us. By the time we left for the beach, we had our cooler full of ice; we had juice, soda, fried chicken, rolls, sandwiches, and all types of fruits—oh, and a camera, too. We got dressed in our jeans and T-shirts, packed up our backpacks, and were on our way for a full day of fun.

Some days, we went to our friend Paula's house. Paula had a big house and lived within the sugar cane area in Clarendon, far from where we got off the bus. Walking all the way to Paula's house was a part of the adventure. When we reached her home, we gathered wood to make a fire and roasted hot dogs on sticks. Someone's finger always got burned, and we always started giggling. Or someone's stick always broke, and their franks burned too much. We always had a good laugh over something.

We all had one thing in common: We were focusing on a good education and having fun while not having a care in the world. We didn't pay much attention to having relationships or sex. We weren't nerds or geeks; in fact, all of the girls were popular, and I think we were all shy, scared of broken relationships and being the center of "locker-room" talk. Since we were not having sexual relationships with the boys, we were very close to them. Judith, Jackie, and I had the best relationships with the boys at school; they were like our brothers.

At the end of one summer, we had a big party because we thought we still hadn't had enough fun. Of course, the party was the Peart house. Mr. Peart gave us money to purchase some of the food, but we didn't have any music. Tracy, Jackie's next-door neighbor, had a companion set, so we borrowed it for the event. Tracey, Judith, and I struggled bringing the set from Tracey's house to Judith's, but we eventually got it there and back safe and sound. The party was simple—music, dancing, food, and laughter. We invited our friends, their friends, boyfriends, brothers, sisters, and even their mothers. We even invited some of our teachers. We had so much food that the next morning, we were oozing leftovers.

When we went back to school, we couldn't stop talking about the summer. But we didn't need to wait until summer to have fun; we had fun at school with every project we completed. Our school planned trips each year, which we participated in from time to time. We always made big events out of our school trips. Judith, Jackie, and I bought matching shirts to wear with our jeans, got all dressed up at the Pearts' house, and stopped by the photo studio to take pictures before we reported to school for the trips.

I was even included in the Pearts' family reunions. I was a part of almost every celebration in that family. Mr. Peart planned annual family excursions to any of the island's resort beaches, and I was often included as well. When the sisters and I started having boyfriends, getting married, having children, and taking on new jobs, the dynamics of our relationship changed somewhat, but we always had a bond among us.

The relationship I had with the Pearts filled an enormous gap in my life, but I always felt something significant was missing. Even though life with my friends was exciting, it couldn't replace the need I had for a relationship with my sisters and brother at home, where I always felt I didn't belong. I loved my siblings, and as my relationships at school and with the Pearts grew, I spent less and less time at home. As a result, conflict with my siblings lessened.

Because I was naturally a talker, whenever I went to exciting events, I went home afterward and spilled my guts to my sisters and brother, blow by blow, dramatizing the events as I told the stories. They laughed at my jokes, and I encouraged them to see whatever play I saw or go wherever I went. One weekend, Janet, Judith's older sister, brought us to see the Oliver Samuels show. It was my first time attending a play. I thought it was so much fun. I told my sisters and brother about it and encouraged them to go to the next play. To get them interested, I started naming the people from the community who attended the play, but they never went.

At this point, since the conflict between my siblings and me was significantly lessened, I started to ask myself whether I was the problem in the family. So I made an effort to spend more time with them. Unfortunately, the unkind and embarrassing comments started again, and I retreated back into my room. My father always found our altercations amusing, and my mother, as usual, had no response. Sometimes I had to "psych myself up" before I left my room to join them and tell myself that no matter what they said, I was not going to move. From that point on, when they poked fun at me, I would just sit there, sometimes laughing at their insults. I remember times when I stood in front of them and actually made performances of their jokes, and they all joined in. Afterward, I thought I had won the battle and that I was probably the problem—that my staying away to avoid the conflict was the reason for the gap between us. But one common element in any relationship is that no matter how much one person wants the relationship to work, it's impossible if the other party doesn't want it as well. I alone couldn't bridge the gap between us, but they didn't see a problem because they were all bonded together. I was the one who was all alone. So, once again, I went back to keeping my distance, and again, it solved all the problems.

An air of uneasiness and a line of separation always existed between me and the rest of the family. The more I tried to survive outside of the family and create a world where I could be happy, the more my brother and sisters made that task difficult. At church, they taunted me and told my friends private and embarrassing moments from my home life. Eventually, I started to confide in Miss Morris, one of my teachers at school. I knew I needed to tell someone what was happening in my house, but my family had projected such a perfect image that I felt no one would believe me. When I told Miss Morris how I was treated at home, she provided me with more comfort and escape. I started spending weekends and holidays at her house. Since she didn't have any children of her own, when she went someplace, sometimes she took me along. Miss Morris was a member of the Lion's Club. On one particular holiday, she brought me to an outreach program. I started spending considerable time with her and her friends.

Home life got progressively worse, and I wrote my mother a letter to let her know how I felt. I placed the letter on the dining-room table one morning before I went to school. After she read the letter, she said that she was going to ask the pastor at church for help. But she never did, and that was the last of the letter. I continued to spend more and more time out of the house. I spent weekends and even Christmas holidays from home with anyone who would have me.

I knew what I wanted to achieve in life, and as long as my friends were going in the same direction, I spent weekends at their homes. It was not until I started writing this book that I realized how much time I really spent away from my family. This should have been a red flag to my parents or anyone close to them. No one else I knew spent so much time out of their home.

Christine, another friend of mine in high school, lived in Poorus, Manchester, with her grandparents on a farm. She was the only child living there, and we became friends. Sure enough, I started going to her house on weekends, and when I wasn't at her house, she was at mine. Ironically, my parents didn't have a problem with my friends coming to the house, so most of the time, when I was home, a friend was with me.

Sometime after I started visiting Christine's house, her uncle moved home to live with them. He was big and tall, the house was old, and the rooms just ran into each other without any passage between them. The bathroom was at the back of the house, and I had to pass her uncle's room, where he was always lying on his bed, before I got to the bathroom. I always raced to the bathroom, locked the door, did whatever I needed to do quickly, and rushed back to Christine's room, because I was afraid her uncle would hold me down and rape me.

After doing my "rush routine" for awhile, one day, I said to myself, "If I am so scared, why am I here?" Of course, the answer came to me as quickly as I had asked the question: "I do not want to be home." Thank God he never even attempted to hurt me, but I realized I could be in a lot of trouble if I ever spent a weekend with the wrong family.

I was always away from home whenever the opportunity presented itself. But I made sure to stay out of trouble and made sure my mother met the families I stayed with. Whenever I went anywhere, I made sure my mother knew exactly where I was going, who I was going with, and when I was coming home, because I wanted her to trust me.

I remember going to Christine's house one particular weekend, and it started to rain on the Sunday I was supposed to come home. It rained intermittently throughout the day. Even though Christine's grandmother thought I should stay until the following day, I told her that my mother was expecting me to be home. As soon as the rain stopped in the afternoon, Christine and I grabbed our umbrellas, and she started to walk me to the bus stop to catch a bus home. By the time we reached the bus stop, though, the rain started really coming down, so she again suggested I stay with her and just go to school with her the next day. But I reminded her again that my mother was expecting me home. We waited for nearly two hours and could not get a bus.

As the evening approached, I stood out in the rain under my umbrella and started flagging down cars. I was picked up by what seemed like a family—two ladies, a man, and a child, if I remember correctly. When they asked why I was standing in the rain, I told them I had spent the weekend with my friend and that my mother was expecting me home that day. The driver of the car told me he heard on the radio that it was an "all-island rain," so my mother would understand if I stayed until the next day.

And as it turned out, when I arrived home, I found out the driver of the car was right. As soon as I arrived, my mother asked, "Why didn't you stay with Christine until Monday?"

I replied, "I told you I was coming home on Sunday, and that is why I came home in the rain." I thought that always doing everything right would make me accepted in my home. Unfortunately, I discovered that I could never do anything that was good enough to please them. I never felt that I belonged, and I was hoping for something to happen that would finally bond me to my own family.

Ultimately, I spent more and more time away from home, always making sure that while I was away, I did the right things, always walking the straight line and never going against the family standard. As soon as school was out for summer break, I packed to go somewhere to somebody's house, someone, anyone, who didn't blame me for everything, somewhere I could go about the day without looking over my shoulder, somewhere where people could tell me when I was wrong and resolve a conflict in a healthy manner. The surroundings were never important. I only went to get away from my own home where I didn't belong.

The greatest thing that a man can do
is to give birth to himself.

Chapter 3 ❦

Birth Order

I started psychoanalyzing before I knew "psychoanalysis" was a word. I had already established that my brother and sisters had an unhealthy relationship with me because of the difference in our ages and the order in which we were born. I also realized that each of us were different and special in our own way. My sister, Grace, was the oldest. She was neat and nurturing, always in the kitchen with my mother cooking and always making repairs around the house. Rocky was the second child. He was a very talented singer and incredibly focused, ambitious, and the ultimate go-getter. Dawn was the ultimate middle child, a diva and people pleaser who was always wearing the latest fashions and hairstyles. She was not interested in sports or politics and was not as active in church as the rest of us.

I was the last child and very opinionated. I paid little attention to detail. I was also terribly emotional and had a good sense of humor. My mother was an only child. She was very thin-skinned—easily offended—and had hardly any sense of humor at all. But like Dawn, she was a people pleaser. My father was the firstborn son of thirteen children; he was the third child with two older sisters. My father was the ultimate "Fidel Castro," because he became very angry with anyone who didn't agree with his points of view. He dominated my mother and siblings, but oh no, not me! Did I say I was opinionated? Yes, I was always asking, "Why?" This was one of the reasons I was so unpopular at home; I was not afraid of anyone, not even my father.

The experiences we have in life cause us to behave the way we do. Having spent so much time outside of my home, I was not afraid of anyone. The more my family hurt me, the more resilient I became. The more our personalities clashed, the more I studied us. I knew our behavior had to do in part with the order in which we were born, so I started to look at the dynamics of other families. After I graduated high school, I studied social work at the University of the West Indies. Soon afterward, I found a book written by Dr. Kevin Leighmon that exclusively discussed the effects of birth order on an individual. The findings of his studies fit my family like a glove—well, almost.

My father, as the firstborn son, displayed the characteristics of a first child; he was a controlling perfectionist who kept things in order. My mother, the only child, was also a perfectionist, but she made decisions to please others and was very concerned about what other people thought. Grace was the first child and naturally displayed the perfectionist protective personality. Rocky was the first son who was also a perfectionist. Dawn, in the middle, wasn't very concerned with perfection but wanted to please others. Then came the last child who dared to be different, not afraid of anyone—a far different personality from the rest of the family. The more I read about birth order, the more I understood why our family had the kind of relationship we did.

I learned early that my mother was afraid of many things because she always said she didn't have any brothers and sisters to defend her. She was also afraid of my father's large family. My great-grandmother gave my father a small house on a large piece of land, but my mother refused to live in it because she was worried that his large family would cause her trouble. So they bought a house far from my father's family, which made her feel safe. My mother stayed very much to herself when we were children. Only in the latter years of her life did she have close personal friends. The only relative she had was her mother who lived in Canada when we were young children. But she was a tough person, because she wanted the best life possible for her children and made the effort to take advantage of the limited opportunities she had.

As a young wife and mother, she tried to get herself involved in activities to pass her time and learn a skill while doing so. She played an active role in our community's home economics project the government had initiated. I remember her coming home and experimenting with new recipes she learned at the club. She made mango jams and pumpkin fritters. She tried her best as a mother with limited means to give us small treats now and then, such as puzzle books, jacks, and card games, in addition to the basic necessities.

My father, on the other hand, was very domineering. He spoke to my mother as if she had no rights at all. My sisters and brother were afraid of him, but I never was. When the children in our community were having fun, my older siblings stayed home. We lived about half an hour from the beach where groups of young people went on holidays. My sisters were not allowed to go with their friends, but our father sometimes let us go with friends of the family. There was a time when I only observed what was going on in our home without ever taking any action, but as I grew older, I refused to tolerate my father's drastic disciplinary mentality. I understand that he was trying to protect us, but we also needed to socialize. I never disrespected my father; I learned early that there was a right way and a wrong way to solve problems.

At a harvest celebration one Sunday afternoon, the kids were standing outside church talking to friends. I stood chatting and laughing with a group of my girlfriends. We started talking with three boys when my father spotted me. In a very stern way, he called me to him and prepared to take the family home. I went, of course; I was not going to disrespect my father. But when we reached home, I said to him, "You saw me talking with the girls, and it was not a problem for you, but the moment you saw me talking to the boys, you had a problem. Dad, we all go to school, we are teenagers, and it is natural that we have things to talk about."

When Dawn went to school in Kingston and met her boyfriend, she asked me to tell our parents. When Rocky was planning to put a proposal to my father, he asked me to help him negotiate with him.

Dad and I began having long, deep conversations and developed a close relationship as I grew older. I enjoyed his sense of humor. And I came to see my brother and sisters as my role models. I always wanted to be the best person I could be, and for me, that included learning to successfully relate to others and take care of myself. I always learned from the positive elements in their lives and used the negative experiences as a guard against making the same mistakes.

After my sisters left home to go to school in Kingston, Rocky and I became close because we were the only two siblings left at home. Our lives changed as we matured. I started attending church again, and Rocky, who was a remarkably talented singer, became part of a group that performed at other churches. I would tag along at his performances. By this time, life was great at home. My sisters would come home for a weekend, and we'd enjoy each other's company. Rocky and I spent considerable time together talking about politics, sports, and current events. I shared my school textbooks with him. When he wasn't working, I read the daily newspapers and gave him ideas of places to apply and helped him complete job applications. Unfortunately, the relationship with Grace never changed. She always acted as if she had a vendetta against me, but I tried my best to ignore her.

I eventually went away to school at Knox. While I was there, I had no family problems because contact was very limited. My sisters and I all went home on certain weekends, but many times, we didn't go home on the same weekend. As a result, when we eventually saw each other, we had a lot of catching up to do. During this time, everything was great for everyone.

As I studied the way my siblings behaved, I began to compare them to my cousins who were living with us and discovered striking similarities. My oldest cousin, my older sister, my brother, and my father were all perfectionists. My cousin, who was the middle child, along with my middle sister Dawn, were secretive and pretended to be people they weren't in order to please others. And my cousin's younger brother, Dave, and I were both courageous and not afraid of anyone. He defended himself against any of his school's bullies. We were also both very outspoken and had a good sense of humor.

One evening while we were all at home, Dave's older brother, Prince, started to beat him. He complained to my parents, and my father told Prince that it was fine for him to beat Dave because he was older, just like he had told my older siblings that it was okay for them to beat me.

I said to my father, "Prince is not old enough to discipline his little brother."

Angry that I was undermining his authority, he shouted to Prince, "Listen to me, Prince, any time Dave does anything wrong, slap him; you are the older one!"

"Over my dead body!" I yelled. "Prince is only ten; he cannot decide what is right or wrong for his brother."

My father and I went to war, but I was not going to back down; to me, it was personal. Nobody stood up for me when my older brother and sisters were beating me, and I wasn't going to let the same thing happen to my cousin. We had a shouting match, and no one in the house intervened. I was not afraid of my father. He may have been the man of the house, and I may have been only seventeen, but he was wrong, and I was not going to look away. For days afterward, everyone in the house avoided me, and my father and I did not speak for weeks.

I realized it can be unbearably difficult for the last child in the family to survive the harassment of older siblings. And the situation can become abusive and hateful if there is no strong parental intervention. All four of us had different personalities, but that didn't mean we couldn't get along. What was missing was that our parents didn't allow us to respect each other's differences. Because my siblings were always complaining about me and my parents never intervened, they grew up believing that everything I did was wrong. After years of this belief being learned and reinforced, it grew stronger and stronger with time.

I was not the perfect child. I got into mischief as any other child does, but I was not a bad child. I didn't expect my parents to look the other way when I was out of line. But letting my siblings beat me was totally out of line.

My parents may have thought that by looking the other way, they maintained peace in the home, but instead, they only created a bigger mess. By allowing me to always be out of the house, my siblings thought I was given a privilege that they never received, which led them to believe that I was spoiled. In reality, however, my parents only allowed me out of the house because it suited them.

When two people love each other they work together always, two against the world, a little company.

Chapter 4 🍂

Boy Meets Girl

As the years passed, all of us kids matured, graduated school, left home, married, and had children. I was the only one, however, to have children without being married. I met my boyfriend, Ian, while I was working at my first job at Munroe College in St. Elizabeth. He was in his final year at the University of the West Indies in Trinidad where he was completing his bachelor's degree in chemical engineering. We met in late May 1997 when he returned home for the summer holidays. He lived near Munroe, so after we met, he started coming to see me there for the next few weeks. After I went home to Clarendon in July 1997, we began to talk on the phone and visited each other for the rest of the summer. He went back to school for his final year, and I went to work in Kingston.

After he left, I thought, "Well, I guess it was just a summer relationship." But he called me at work, from Trinidad, the same week he left, so I thought that was pretty special. We started communicating on a regular basis, and it felt as if the relationship was more than just a summer fling. He even wrote me a few letters. Later in the year, he came home for Christmas, and I picked him up at the airport.

We had a great Christmas together, and the bond between us became even stronger. After he went back to school in January for the last semester, we were on the phone all the time. Many times, he called me in the middle of the night after he finished studying. He returned to his parents' home and started working at the bauxite plant in the parish in July 1998 after graduation.

He came to see me religiously every Friday evening and left on Monday morning, and it felt like we were living together. If there was a holiday in the week, he was back for that day. If he had to work for the weekend, he picked me up on Friday evening and took me to work with him early Saturday morning. Then he took me home that Sunday evening so I could go to work Monday morning.

Unfortunately, since we spent so much time together, I began to see the real Ian, and there were many things I did not like. When he came home from work on Friday evenings, he fell into a routine. He arrived home, ate dinner, watched the news, took a shower, and went to bed. Then he got up every Sunday; watched cricket on television; read the newspaper; ate breakfast, lunch, and dinner; took a shower; and went to bed. Then he left for work Monday morning.

The hardest time in our relationship came during the first few months after he returned home from college, because he did nothing around the house, and we never went out. On Friday evening, when he came home, I always had a meal cooked for him. Before Ian and I met, I never cooked on Fridays. I always ate out or just had a snack.

One Friday, I decided not to cook, and when Ian came home, I told him that we could just go to the mall and have something to eat at the food court. He replied, "My mother always had my food cooked when I came home."

I started to laugh and said, "I am not your mother."

But we went to the mall and had dinner, and Ian enjoyed himself. Afterward, we started spending quite a few evenings at the mall eating dinner.

I kept telling him that we needed to go out, but he said we didn't have the money. I told him that we didn't need a lot of money to go to a movie or the beach. My girlfriend Judith called me one Saturday and asked us if we wanted to go to Gordon Park with her and her boyfriend, Mark. While I was still on the phone, I told Ian that Judith and Mark were going to the park and they wanted us to come along. He said that we didn't have any money to go, and again, I told him that we didn't need any money and that we were going just to get out of the house and have fun for a day. I had to give the phone to him and let Mark convince him. We had so much fun that day. We fished in an enormous fishing pond, and we caught so many that we had to give some away—that was the highlight of the day.

For months after Ian came home, we were constantly in some sort of disagreement as we tried to fit into each other's lives. I told him that either we had to go our separate ways, or we could try to work out our relationship, but I wasn't going to continue arguing.

We had a long talk, and I told him that I expected us to go out sometimes. He said I should remember that he did not have as much exposure as I did, and I should try to understand that. I told him that I did not like the fighting, and if we decided to stay together, we should try to work out our differences.

We started going out, and our relationship started growing. Ian started coming home on Friday evenings and saying, "Okay, get dressed, we're going to the movies." Then we went to the multiplex and flipped a coin to decide which movie to see. Sometimes we got up in the morning and went to the beach. This whole experience taught me that if we choose to work out differences in a relationship, it can grow in spite of the differences.

For almost two years after that talk, we didn't have any major quarrels. We had little disagreements here and there, but we always worked them out. Other things began to concern me after about three years into the relationship. Ian and I were a working couple in our late twenties, and Ian was not making any future plans for us. I felt the need for more stability in my own life and in the relationship as well. I wanted to start planning for our marriage and household.

Ian was working almost two hours from where I lived, and I thought it was time for us to move closer. The weekend arrangement was growing old and tiring. I wanted to have a baby, and I also wanted to go back to school. At the beginning of 2000, I told Ian how I felt about the relationship.

Even though I started to feel that I was the only one in this relationship, I didn't want to pressure Ian in a direction he didn't want to go. So, after Ian and I talked, I decided to leave the relationship. We both cried about it. I told him I wanted to move to England to work and go to school. We both made plans for the move, and about ten days before my departure, I found out that I was pregnant. We were both so excited, and I wondered if it was fate that we should be together.

But after I got pregnant, I panicked. This was the real thing! I was going to have a baby! I was going to be a mother! Each day, I woke up scared. What if something should happen to me to while I was alone in my apartment? The first few weeks of my pregnancy, I lost my appetite, but Ian always encouraged me to eat. I thought the reason I had to force myself to eat was that I was afraid of being a mother. I thought about holding that little person in my arms and being totally responsible for him or her. I was afraid I would wake up one morning and find myself ill and not know what to do. I told Ian how scared I was, and we decided I would move back to my parents' home. We were both happy that we would be closer to each other.

My due date was January 8, 2001, so we decided I wouldn't go back to work after the Christmas holidays. My parents didn't drive, so we thought that after the holidays, he'd come and get me so that I would be with him when it was time for me to go to the hospital. And even though I was pregnant, Ian and I still went everywhere together, like we had before. When I was six months pregnant, he wanted to take me to a cricket match, but I told him to go without me because I might get uncomfortable and ruin the game for him.

After I moved back home, I felt better because my mother was there every time I needed someone. She took me to the doctor every time I felt something unusual. Actually, I had a very good pregnancy—no morning sickness, no cravings, none of the regular occurrences that pregnant women complain about.

I never thought I needed to ask for my parents' permission to move home; I just told them that I was coming. No matter how long you're away from home, you think you'll always belong there, and you never think to discuss moving back. When my siblings and I were all living at home, I was the only one ever to stand up to my father. After we all left, he was a completely different person. During this time, he told me about his childhood, his early days as an adult, and how proud he was of us.

Our father loved to see all of us come home on Sundays and park our cars in the yard. There were times when one of us picked up the others so we arrived in only one car. But somehow, Dad was always happier when we arrived separately. He spoke about his children all the time, and it made us happy that we made our parents proud.

When I moved back home, however, he started to change little by little. Even though I didn't ask my parents' permission to move home, I did tell them that I would be there for a while, and as soon as I had my baby, I would get my own place. My father began to behave differently. He didn't direct any of his anger toward me; it was always toward my mother and Kerri and Lindon, the two adopted children who lived with them. At first, my mother and the children were amused at his behavior. Kerri and Lindon started to call him a name to match the way he was carrying on. When they saw him coming, they shouted, "Here comes Mr. Thunder." And we just looked at each other as we braced ourselves for his outburst.

After awhile, I didn't think it was funny anymore. I knew there was something else to his behavior. I started to wonder if my father was angry because I was there and was expressing it in another way.

The day after Christmas, I didn't see or hear from Ian. The day after that, there was no sign of Ian. But in the middle of the night, one of his friends dropped him off. He told me he was coming from a dance. I was sitting at the kitchen table when he came home. I asked him, "Why haven't you called me for the past two days? You were supposed to come and get me two days ago!" He did not answer. I said, "You know that my parents don't drive, and I can have the baby any time now because I only have two weeks until my due date."

He was silent the whole time I was talking to him. I got up from the table and went to bed, but I couldn't sleep. About twenty minutes later, I went to the bathroom and realized my underwear was wet. I went to my mother's room and told her, and she told me to put on a sanitary napkin and go back to bed.

When the sanitary napkin was soaked twenty minutes later, I realized that my water had broken, so we went to the hospital. After examining me, the doctors told me I wasn't having any contractions even though my water had broken. They tried to induce labor, but nothing happened, so they delivered my daughter, Afreka, by C-section. I was in the hospital for about a week, and Ian took a week off from work so that he could stay with me and the baby.

I sensed a change in Ian, but I thought it was because of the birth of the baby and the fact that we were not at our own place. He was still attentive to me and Afreka, and he brought me to my doctor's appointments. Two weeks after Afreka was born, I started the process of buying a house even though I was still uncertain about our lives together when I went to pick up the form from the National Housing Trust to apply for the house. But Ian walked into the living room as I was filling out the form and holding the baby in my lap at the same time. He took the form and told me to take care of the baby while he finished filling out the form. Again, I thought that it must be fate for us to be together, because I was about to fill out the form without his name and he completed the form with both of our names on it.

I submitted the application, but by the time Ian and I were called for an interview, the houses were all sold. So instead, we were offered land and the money to build our own home. Ian and I thought this was even better, but it also meant staying at my parents' house longer than I expected.

We closed the deal on the land, received the money from the National Housing Trust, and started to build. Building the home took more than a year. While my father still wasn't complaining about me being there, he was constantly upset with my mother and the children. At this point, nobody found it funny anymore. My father was never the one to hit us when we were young, at least not me—my siblings may have a different story. But now he was throwing things at the children. When he started behaving badly, I found a quiet place and calmed him down. But he never changed.

My father lived a respectful life and was well respected in our community. He was on the church board and was the head deacon. The entire time we lived at home, people in our community only had great things to say about us. He was proud that none of us came home with the usual problems children had at our age—no teenage pregnancy, no drugs, and no promiscuity—nothing that caused parents to feel ashamed. Instead, we were everything that made parents proud.

We went to school, passed exams, went to college, got married, and then had children. But since I was the only one to have children out of wedlock and was living at home, they couldn't hide from it. They saw me every day, as did our friends. This situation was nothing for our parents to feel proud of, so they couldn't deal with it.

Not a day would go by when my father wouldn't be outraged at something. One evening, he came home and saw the dishes were not washed and ordered Kerri to wash them. I told him it was not her evening to do the dishes because it was Lindon's turn. But he insisted that Kerri do the dishes right then and didn't care whose evening it was. Because Kerri knew it was not her evening, she went reluctantly, looking for my response. I nodded and told her to go, thinking I would have Lindon do the dishes on one of Kerri's evenings. So we did what my father wanted, without it being unfair to any of the children.

My father threw a giant stick at Kerri, and she came crashing into me while I had Afreka in my hand. All three of us landed on the sofa in the living room. When I saw the size of the stick, I thought, "What would have happened if it had caught any of us?" When he looked in the hallway, he only saw Kerri. But if a stick that size had caught my baby, I am sure she would be dead. I realized we had a problem, but we couldn't change him.

Without telling Ian what was happening at home, I started to push for the completion of the house. As I received the checks from the National Housing Trust, I purchased the building materials at Epic Hardware. I had become a regular customer; they set up an aggressive account for me. The trust did not give us the money to build the house all at once. The money was issued in stages. Whenever one phase of the building was finished, we requested more money to go to the next phase. It took anywhere from two weeks to a month to receive the funds each time I requested more. The account I set up at Epic Hardware allowed me to credit material until I received my next check. That way, I could push the work on the house while the check was being processed. During this time, Ian and I would sometimes have to use our paychecks to pay the builders.

When Afreka was six weeks old, we went to spend a week with Ian's parents. Afreka was not eating well, so Ian's mother suggested I take her to see the doctor. So I drove Ian's truck to the doctor's office. That same night, he went to his grandmother's house after he came home from work, something he always did. But when I woke up the next morning, I realized he didn't come home. Even though I had mixed emotions, I was sure he had a very good explanation for not coming home.

He couldn't have spent the whole night with another woman, because I was only at his mother's house for a week, and if he was cheating on me, that would have been bad enough, but to sleep out while I was at his mother's house would make it so much more disrespectful. He finally came home and burst into the room laughing. I started laughing, too. I said, "Tell me that somebody died, because there must be a very good reason for you to stay out all night."

He answered, "Oh! Yes, the truck was out of gas. I told you to put gas in the tank, but you didn't."

"So where did you get gas to come home so early in the morning?" I asked.

"There is a gas station not too far from here that is open early in the mornings," he replied.

"You know what, Ian?" I said. "I believe you, because you could not be cheating on me and stay out all night because that would be downright disrespectful. Anyway, I need some new clothes so let's go shopping."

So, we had a good time at the mall. But afterward, Ian's behavior continued to change, and I knew something was going on. An air of uneasiness continued to exist between us that I had never experienced before, and I wasn't sure how to deal with it. Our conversation was reduced to talking about my daughter and the house. We weren't having sex because my doctors told me I needed to wait about three months after the operation before resuming sexual activity.

Even his weekend visits were becoming shorter and shorter. Instead of coming to see me on Friday nights, he came Saturday afternoons and left on Sunday evenings. He'd wake up early and head out saying he was going to look at the progress of the building of our new home. This was the first time he didn't want me to come with him when he was going somewhere. Taking our daughter with us wouldn't have been a problem.

My parents grew a lot of mangoes, and Jim, one of the men who worked on our house, asked me for some. I picked a whole box and gave it to Ian to give to him. But when I went to see the house the following week, Jim asked me for the mangoes. I told him that I sent a whole box with Ian the Sunday before, but Jim said Ian never came. Yet he was gone all day. So where else could he go?

I found it odd that he was going to see the house even during the slow periods when nothing new was being built. When I asked him why he was going to the house when the builders hadn't built anything new for the past few weeks, he replied that he was just excited about the house so he was going there to hang out.

At one point, I had to go to Kingston on business, so I decided I would take Afreka and stay near Dawn for a few days. After Ian brought us into Kingston, it only took a few days to complete my business there, but I ended up staying for two weeks because Ian kept coming up with excuses for not picking us up.

I could feel us growing apart, but I didn't know what to do about it. I was planning to leave Ian, but I thought I would talk to someone about it before making such a drastic decision. So, I spoke to a friend who was a bit older than I was, and she told me that men act that way when they are cheating. She told me that this was going to be one of the challenges in the relationship because we had been together for so long. She said that every relationship goes through difficulties, and since men are cowards, he may not tell me he wants the relationship to end. She told me that I would know based on his actions when it was time to leave. She said that right now, he might have just been behaving as he was because he was in this new relationship. In the end, she told me I needed to confront the situation.

I went back to work in May 2001. Ian was getting ready to leave for Louisiana on a business trip. Before he left, I confronted him about my suspicion. "Ian, I know you are cheating on me," I said.

He hesitated for a minute then replied, "How did you know?"

"You just admitted to me that you are cheating," I answered.

He went silent.

I said to him, "I knew situations like this could happen. But now that I am faced with it, I do not know to handle it." So I asked him if he wanted to end our relationship, and he said he wanted to be with his family. He did not have much more to say.

He left for Louisiana at the end of June, and he called me every day. He was very excited about his trip and wanted me to come and be with him. So I left Jamaica for New York in July, and he was anxious for me to come and spend some time with him. Before I left, he mailed my ticket to my uncle's house. I left for Louisiana the day after I got to New York.

When he picked me up from the airport, he was so excited to see me. He showed me around New Orleans before we headed to the hotel. When I arrived, he immediately started shopping for me. He took the weekend off from work and didn't return to work until Monday night. It was like our lives were back to normal. I took the time again to talk to him about the affair he was having, but again, he denied it. I said, "Well, you need to end the relationship that you are not having."

When he returned to Jamaica, we were back to our old selves again. We were going out again, and the house was now at its final stage of building. I found out I was pregnant about three weeks after he returned. I was so surprised at my pregnancy I couldn't bring myself to tell anyone. I had just begun to lose the baby fat from having my daughter when I got pregnant again. For months, Ian was the only one I had told. But he told me to tell my friends because he felt I needed support from them. I was nearly three months along when I told my friends at work, but they really thought I was joking. Ian told my parents and my sister, who told the rest of the family.

Everyone in the family made fun of the situation, saying I had given away my maternity clothes and I needed to get them back. Grace said, "As a matter of fact, after you have the baby this time, you should put up your maternity clothes to make sure you don't give them away again. You look like you're going to follow in your grandmother's footsteps." My grandmother had thirteen children.

As the New Year approached, my house was finally well on its way to completion. The structure of the house was completed in December 2001, and we moved into the house in May 2002, just a few weeks before my son, Dakhari, was born. My sisters had a baby shower for me, which I was not expecting since they had given me one for my daughter just the year before. They held it at my house so they had to tell me beforehand, in order for me to get my house ready for visitors.

Before I moved out of my parents' home, I sat them down and told them I was very grateful that they allowed me to stay while I was pregnant and for the birth of my daughter. I also pointed out my father's behavior and told them they needed to try to get along better with each other and the children. I reminded my father that my mother sometimes had problems with her blood pressure, and he should try to calm down. My father left for Georgia shortly afterward.

After we moved into our new house, Ian started acting strangely again. He changed his cell phone number but didn't give me the new number. As time grew closer for the birth of Dakhari, he started coming home late or not at all. So I said to him, "How can you not come home when I am in a state like this?"

He replied, "If anything happens, call Paula." She was my neighbor and had a baby of her own and two older children, and besides, we had just met after we all moved into our new home.

After our son was born, Ian continued to stay out nights. My daughter was only eighteen months old, so I had two babies to deal with. He usually came home after I put the babies to bed. One night, I was tidying up the living room after the babies went to sleep when he came home. We talked in the living room for a while, and then I went to take a shower. As soon as I turned the water on, I heard him talking on his cell phone. So, I turned the water off, and I heard him saying, "I will call you back tomorrow. I will call you back tomorrow." The next morning, I picked up his phone and dialed the number. A woman answered.

I asked her, "What is going on between you and Ian?"

"We are having a relationship," she replied.

I confronted Ian about it. He said he didn't know which woman I called, and that anyone could tell me anything, but that he was not having any relationship with anyone. Nonetheless, he always found an excuse to leave the house every Saturday, and he couldn't even take time to attend his own son's christening.

Exactly one week after the birth of my son, I received a call from Rocky, who congratulated me, and we talked for a while. Then he said that Dada told him I encouraged Mama to adopt a child without his permission or approval, and he was very stressed about it. Rocky's wife was listening on the other phone in their home and said, "I'm going to be very upset if my husband is upset." I was very confused and started trying to remember the events surrounding Lindon's adoption.

I replied, "I did not encourage Mama to adopt. She approached me with her plans, and I asked her why she wanted to do it. Then she told me that ever since all of us left home she wanted a child in the house. She continued to say that she tried to get children to come and live with her, but eventually, they all went back home. So she thought that if she officially adopted, the child would stay with her. I was also a little surprised when she told me about it."

"So if Mama told you that," Rocky continued, "why didn't you tell anyone about it?"

"Because it is not my place to tell everyone else about Mama," I responded. "She is not an invalid. She is quite capable of making her own decisions, and she is the one who should tell her children about her plans. You all should make sure that you communicate with her, too."

Rocky's wife started saying that women my mother's age should not adopt children. My mother started the adoption process when she was in her mid-fifties, and as she approach sixty, I told her that if she didn't get a child in the next few years, she should forget about it.

They carried on and on about teenage boys being difficult to deal with and said that my parents were not strong enough to deal with them. But I told them that as long as we extended our support, it would be easier on them. But they were more focused on the fact that I was the one who encouraged my mother to adopt this child and no one else in the family knew about it. So I suggested to Rocky and his wife that we all pitch in and help. Or if we all thought our parents couldn't really raise the children, we could send them back. But Rocky said, "At this point, the damage is already done. My parents are hurting by that decision you made."

The entire time we were having this conversation, I was thinking back on the details of Lindon's adoption. In the middle of the conversation, I said, "Wait a minute! Dawn and Grace knew about it! Dada knew about it! We all knew about it!"

"You're lying! You're lying!" Rocky shouted. "I spoke to Dawn and she knew nothing about it!"

At that point, the calmness went out of me. I yelled back, "You wait a minute! Boy, you did not just sit up there in Atlanta and call me a liar! Oh no, you didn't!" He continued to speak, so I yelled, "You need to stop right now! Listen to me! Everyone in this family knew about this, and it's not my responsibility to tell everyone about it! Mama is not an invalid, and if she made this decision and you are not in agreement with it, go ask her about it!"

He realized how angry I was and said, "Okay, okay. I am going to call Dawn, and then I'll call you back."

He called back when he couldn't reach Dawn, but this time, we didn't talk for long. The next morning as soon as my babysitter came, I went to my mother's house and said, "Mother, we need to talk." We went into the living room. She sat on the sofa while I took a seat in the chair closest to her. I said, "Now, I want to make sure I don't miss a word or misunderstand anything you said." She look confused, so I continued, "Rocky called me yesterday and accused me of encouraging you to adopt Lindon and said Dada knew nothing about it. Is this true?"

Mother looked puzzled then began to speak. "I discussed it with your father before I started the process," she replied. "The social workers came here and talked to your father. Every once in a while, he asked me if I heard anything from the adoption agency. I thought that was strange because he said he didn't want to deal with any children at this stage in his life, and you brought the boy in his house without his consent." Mother sighed, then she continued, still looking confused, "But even before Lindon came here, we were trying to get a boy from Manchester. We discussed the whole thing, and he knew the day I was going for the boy. The day I came back without him, he wanted to know what happened. Your father was very disappointed. He asked me what happened, and I told him that the boy's mother had a lot of children and could not manage them, but the father of the boy she was giving to me turned up and said he would take care of his child. There was another boy in the yard, and one lady said to me, 'Lady, you can take that one if you want, because he doesn't have a mother or father.' Another man said, 'Lady, don't carry that boy to your yard because he is a thief.' But your father still wanted to take him because he figured the boy was probably stealing because he did not have anything to eat. So, he thought maybe when he got enough to eat, he would not steal."

I sat back on the sofa, smiled, and shook my head. This story was news to me. At least thus far, it sounded like my father knew enough about this adoption. I then asked my mother, "What about Dawn and Grace? Did they know?"

She turned to me and said, "Lisa, you forget that the first time I went to the adoption agency in Kingston, I stayed overnight at Dawn's house that Sunday, and O'Neil brought me to the office Monday morning."

I said, "Okay, then it sounds to me as if the whole family knew about this adoption." But for some reason that I could not understand, I was blamed for all of this. Why would my father tell my brother a lie about me?

As much as it is possible be at piece with all men.

Chapter 5 ♥

Conflict Resolution

Finding a scapegoat and passing the buck was my family's way of resolving conflict. My father ruled with an iron fist, yet he couldn't resolve conflict. When I was a small child, my oldest sister and brother had a problem they wanted my father to solve. My father told them all they needed to do was not speak to each other and the problem would be solved. That became the family standard for everyone. But when we were at church or any other public place, we spoke to each other so we could create the illusion of the perfect family. I recently found a quotation that said, "Good families are usually worse than others."

As long as two or more people continue to live together under the same roof, conflict is inevitable. Conflict can begin over a new family member, for example, because children often feel their relationship with their parents is threatened by the new arrival. Each sibling is jealous of the other, because they want to know that they matter to their parents. Working things out with your children gives them important skills like cooperation and being able to see another person's point of view. I have two small children of my own; the moment I brought my son home, the conflict started.

My daughter was only eighteen months old when my son was born, but her place was in my arms right up to the time I went into the hospital. I remember when I came home with her brother, I put him on the bed for them to get acquainted. Afreka jumped up on the bed, their eyes locked in silence, and then she named him "Anum." At night, when she was ready to be held in my lap, the fun was over. She stood before me and pointed at the baby saying, "Mommy, put it down, the baby, put it down, the baby." I had to explain to her that after Dakhari fell asleep, I would pick her up. We went through that same dialogue every night. She always followed me to the crib when I put her brother down. When I turned around, there she was with her hand up in the air ready for me to pick her up, and for the rest of the night, it was Afreka and Mommy time.

One of the ways of relating to a person is knowing him; knowledge is the essence of a good relationship. We may remember the story in the Bible where Balaam was riding his donkey when an angel appeared to the donkey. Balaam started beating the donkey, but the animal couldn't move past the angel. So his master kept on beating him, but he could not pass the angel. So the angel spoke to Balaam and essentially said, "You have been with this donkey for more than forty years, and the animal has always been faithful to you. So don't you think something is causing it not to move?"

While I was a student, I had two friends, Heather and Janice, who took the same classes with me. One day after class, we walked across campus to get something to eat. Janice and I decided to get sandwiches, but Heather said she wanted chicken and rice. Heather would have to go across campus to get her chicken and rice in the cafeteria while Janice and I would just go to the sandwich shop close by. So I said, "Go on—we will come and eat with you in the cafeteria."

The line was long in the sandwich shop, and by the time we reached the cashier, I said, "I think I am going to eat here then head on down to Heather." By the time we sat down to eat, there came Heather with her food, and we all started laughing, but we could have easily had a conflict because I told Heather that we would meet her at the cafeteria. But she assumed that the lines would be long and we would not want to walk to the cafeteria. So, to avoid a conflict, she came back to us. Many conflicts start over incidents just as simple, but in the same way, they can be avoided just as simply as we avoided a fight over lunch. We don't always know how people will react in every situation, so the next best thing is to give the person the benefit of the doubt. That way, if the person is proven right, then we will be happy we gave him or her the benefit of the doubt. If the person is wrong, then you have the opportunity to know how credible he or she really is.

My daughter Afreka was very skinny. She was never a chubby child. I often bought her clothes a size below her age. She started school before she was three, because she was such a chatterbox. Her uniform was a green tunic and white blouse, but on Fridays, she wore a green skirt and white blouse. One Friday, as I got her dressed in her skirt, she said, "Don't wanna wear that, Mommy." I couldn't understand what she was saying, so I picked her up, and she continued, "Don't wanna wear that, Mommy." Then she pointed to her tunic and said, "Wanna wear that." There was something almost compelling about the way she said it, so I put her tunic on her instead of her skirt.

When I brought her to school that morning, I went into her class and told her teacher that she did not want to wear her skirt today even though I couldn't figure out why. The teacher covered her mouth and said, "Oh, my gosh, Miss O'Connor, I forgot to tell you."

I looked at her puzzled and said, "Tell me what?"

She replied, "Last Friday, when she came to school in her skirt, she was playing in the school yard, and her skirt fell off of her. She was so ashamed that she cried and stayed in her classroom the rest of the day."

I was so happy I had given my daughter the benefit of the doubt that day. Playing outside was so important to her. Had I not listened to her, she might have sat in her classroom all day and not played.

Sometimes, the consequences of not giving a person the benefit of the doubt can cause severe harm. I remember watching *Days of Our Lives* a few years ago when Phyllis was married to Jack. Diane and Phyllis were constantly fighting, and Diane planned to burn down Jack's father's house and make it look like Phyllis did it. She dressed up in a wig that resembled Phyllis's hair because she knew that a surveillance camera was at the house. After the deed was done, even though all the evidence pointed to Phyllis, she sat her husband down and told him she did not do it. Jack was the only person who believed her, and that was the only thing she needed to prove her innocence and save her from going to prison. Sometimes, all we need to resolve a conflict is one who believes enough in us to do something about it.

Sometimes conflicts develop from a simple misunderstanding. Within families, misunderstandings frequently occur. Siblings often feel neglected, for example, whenever one is shown more attention than another. In those situations, the other child only needs affirmation from the parents.

One Sunday, I went to my friend's house. She was concerned that the temperature was going to be 27 the next morning, and she wanted a ski mask for her eight-year-old son, Keymar. I asked, "What is a ski mask, and why do you need one for Keymar?" She laughed, and then explained that skiers use ski masks to protect their faces from the wind, and that in the winter, children who ride to school usually wear them to break the wind from their faces. She went into her son's closet and made sure she dressed Keymar in nice warm clothes for the cold weather. We went on the road in search of a ski mask, but we didn't find one. So I said, "Maybe there just aren't any ski masks in Florida."

She called me the following morning, laughing, telling me that her seventeen-year-old son, Andrew, was upset because she had been carrying on about his little brother and wasn't even once concerned about him. She said he mentioned everything she did the day before for Keymar. So, she had to explain the reason she was more concerned about Keymar was because he went to school at 7 a.m., and it was 27 degrees at that time. At 9 a.m., when Andrew went to school, it was 10 degrees warmer. Keymar also rode to school while Andrew just walked to the front of the apartment building to catch his school bus, which had a heater inside.

She continued by telling Andrew that he was seventeen, she didn't usually pick out clothes for a seventeen-year-old, and she had already made sure there were warm clothes in his closet anyhow. She told me that Andrew was always saying she paid more attention to Keymar and acted as if he was not important. But she explained to Andrew that for nine years, he was the only child, and the attention he received as an only child his brother could not get because there were now two of them.

As I hung up the phone, I began to understand more about the dynamics of my family. My parents never took the time to dispel assumptions my siblings had about me being the favorite. Instead, they ignored the whole situation, hoping it would go away. The only thing that allows family members to understand one other is communication.

Listening to how children feel about what is going on in the family is really important. They may not be so demanding if at least they know their parents care about how they feel. In a conflict, parents should allow each child to express his or her feelings about the situation. It's never wise to allow children to constantly call each other names or bully one another. As parents, we would never accept these behaviors from another child who is not a sibling, therefore, we should not allow these behaviors from members of our own families. Remember, issues that are not addressed only lay dormant until they can find a way to rise to the surface.

Love that does not express it self in loving action does not really exist.

Sydney J. Harris

Chapter 6 ❦

Love Is a Verb

If I speak in the tongues of men and of angels, but have not love, I am only a resounding gong or a clanging cymbal. If I have the gift of prophecy and can fathom all mysteries and all knowledge, and if I have a faith that can move mountains, but have not love, I am nothing. If I give all I possess to the poor and surrender my body to the flames, but have not love, I gain nothing.

Love is patient, love is kind. It does not envy, it does not boast, it is not proud. It is not rude, it is not self-selling, it is not easily angered, it keeps no record of wrongs. Love does not delight in evil but rejoices in the truth. It always protects, always trusts, always hopes, always perseveres.

Love never fails. But where there are prophecies, they will cease; where there are tongues, they will be stilled; where there is knowledge, it will pass away. And now these three remain: faith, hope and love. But the greatest of these is love.

1 Corinthians 13:1-13 (NIV)

This scripture passage from the Bible teaches us how we can define love. While acknowledging that love is a verb, an action, this passage mentions so many "actions" that we can take without the action of love, how people give all they have to the poor and surrender their bodies to the flames, yet do not possess love. How can we go to such extremes and still lack love? How could it be possible for anyone to do these things unless it is for anything but the highest form of love? Our Savior, Jesus Christ, gave his life on the cross for us—that is how much he loves us. So is it possible for anyone to lay down his or her life for anything other than love? We have seen many times how suicide bombers blow themselves up to take the lives of themselves and others, thinking they will get some reward. But is that love?

Love can be complex yet very simple; it can be as complex as we want it to be or as simple as we make it. It becomes complex whenever people say they love us and their actions say the opposite. It's as if they say they love us, and we have to take their word for it simply because they say they do. I have loved, and believe me, I know what it feels like. Love is not relative; you either love or you don't. There is one thing I discovered about love: There is very little difference in loving my friends and family than there is in loving someone I am having an intimate relationship with. In writing this chapter, I will have to use my personal feelings and experiences along with quotations from the Bible and other sources to make my point.

One day at work, a coworker told me a story about her daughter. After her daughter graduated from college, she moved to Kingston with a roommate to take a job. Soon after, they started having relational problems, and her daughter soon moved out. After that, she and her roommate did not speak for awhile; however, one day, my friend's daughter called her to tell her that her ex-roommate was out of a job and that she was very concerned. She called back days later to say that her friend found a job and that she was happy, because it was difficult to survive without a job. After my friend hung up the phone, she said to herself, "I have raised my children well."

When someone we care about is facing a difficult situation, even if we are not on speaking terms, we feel their pain. That is love.

I remember when I graduated from dental school. Dawn lived fifteen minutes from the school, and she didn't even show up for my graduation. My mother was away at the time, and when she returned home, I said, "You know, Dawn didn't come to my graduation and didn't even answer the invitation."

Dawn and I didn't speak after that. At the time, Dawn was in her early stages of pregnancy. About three months later, her water broke when she was only seven months along. She was hospitalized while the doctors were trying to save the baby and trying to prolong her pregnancy. The water kept coming, and they had to let her have the baby prematurely. Grace told me what was happening, and even though Dawn and I were not on speaking terms, I was by her side at the hospital. She had bought me a lovely outfit earlier, so I made sure I wore it to the hospital to make her feel good. I stayed with her the whole day, running errands for her as needed.

The Rev. Dr. Martin Luther King, Jr., said, "The true measure of a man is not where he stands in moments of comfort and convenience, but where he stands at times of challenge and controversy." When people attend weddings and baby showers, for example, they are generally pleasant and supportive. When someone we know lands a good job or receives a diploma, we celebrate their achievement. How many of us go to the bookstore to buy a book or card for someone who has stopped going to church or has fallen in with the wrong crowd, is on drugs, or is going through a divorce or a broken relationship. Not many of us are good with words, particularly in those scenarios, but a simple card can sometimes say a thousand words.

Sometimes I get confused when people say they love and don't show it. If you can't show love, it does not exist. William Shakespeare once said, "Love that is not expressed in loving action does not really exist." I truly believe that there can be an absence of love, but that does not necessarily mean hate.

Even though I know my parents don't love me, I am also sure they don't hate me even though they spend their lives being satisfied with saying that they love me. The problem was believing that they did. The actions that accompany the feeling were never seen as a necessary part of the process of loving. Like any living thing that does not exercise, love not accompanied by action will die, and when the occasion arises for you to really take action, you will not be able to stand up to the test, because the act is so out of shape.

When an athlete is scheduled to compete in an event, he will practice for weeks to be sure that his body is ready for the action. If he just gets up to compete on the day of the event without practicing, he is sure to injure himself because of the lack of exercise. The same goes for love: You have to practice it all the time on everyone to keep it alive.

"My little children let us not love in word, neither in tongue: but in deed and in truth" (1 John 3:18 (KJV)).

The greatest love is the one that begins at home. In the words of Mother Teresa, "Love begins at home; it is not how much we do, but how much love we put into that action." Those who are loved at home learn to love themselves, and those who love themselves find it easier to love others.

The children who will many times get ridiculed are the ones who are beaten at home. As a little girl, I had a hard time at church because it was obvious that I was resented by my family. I remember once, my friends were practicing their math skills for the common entrance exam. I didn't participate in the discussion because I didn't do very well at math. As my friends got into their discussion, I said, "Guys, be quiet." Well, Rocky's friend told him I was talking in church. My cousin Katy said to me, "You realize that you are the one they pick on, because they know they couldn't go to Aunt Mer with this." Katy lived with Aunt Mer at the time.

It's amazing how different people look at love and find unique ways to express its concept. An unknown author once said, "Love does not die easily. It is a living thing; it thrives in the face of all life's hazards, save one—neglect."

Ursula Le Guin said, "Love does not just sit there like a stone; it has to be made like a bread, remade all the time made new." The message is simple; it is not possible to have love and do nothing with it, or it will die, not to be necessarily replaced by hate...It will just die.

Love allows us to care for others, hurt if someone we love is hurting, and feel elated if someone has achieved greatness. It also allows us to feel disappointment when our loved ones are facing failure and pain and when we or a loved one has experienced loss, death, or separation. These are products of love. We mold, fold, and taste love when it is the only thing we can reach for, and because we keep holding on, it becomes alive and shaped into a product.

As I went through the separation with my children's father and reached for my family, they were not there. Instead, they turned against me. The biggest puzzle was the fact that my whole world was comprised of Christians. So what could I have done that was so awful that there was absolutely no compassion for someone who was going through the most traumatic time in her life?

I began to look to the Bible and God for my answers. I have sinned, of course, because I am an unwed mother and have two children out of wedlock, but no one is perfect. I still believed the church that I grew up in was not going to fail me, so when the church elder called me one day, I was sure I was going to be refreshed. He joked around for awhile; then he started singing and I joined in. Then he said, "I spoke to your brother, and he said he loves you."

"No, he doesn't," I replied. "If he loved me, he would not try to get my children's father to destroy me the way he did."

He then asked, "Have you ever done anything as a child that you were punished for, but later, you came to accept your family's reasoning?"

I couldn't figure out what it was that I had done to deserve that kind of response. I left a relationship where my children's father was living with somebody else while we were still living together. So, I said to him, "My high school principal, Mr. Preddie, once told me, 'When something is wrong, it is just wrong.' Martin Luther King went a step further by saying, 'Even if everyone around you thinks it is right, it is still wrong.' I realize that I made a choice to go into the relationship with Ian, but it was also his choice to live with two women at the same time. But it was wrong for him to force me to continue to live in the situation after his intentions became clear. It was also wrong for Rocky to try to hurt me when I was trying to leave a life that was no longer nurturing to me and my children and, on top of that, to help Ian try to destroy me."

For me, the message was not clear, but I tried to understand the point the elder was trying to make. Should I have stayed in the situation simply because I made the choice to get involved with him in the first place? The conversation continued, and I said, "My brother could not have loved me and done all the things he did to me."

To this, the leader of the church said, "Are you sure you are not just being biased?" I realized then it was time for me to stop talking. Then he said, "We are going to pray."

I said, "No."

He asked, "You mean you don't want to pray?"

I responded, "Pray if you want, but I will not."

Then, he made one final statement: "*Sinting tan so tan bad*," which is Jamaican for "You are a hopeless case." Afterward, he prayed.

In the *Rhyme of the Ancient Mariner*, Samuel Taylor Coleridge writes:

> He prayeth well that loveth well
> Both man and bird and beast
> he prayeth best who loveth best
> all things great and small.

Many times, people have already judged us in times of trouble. They have already hung us out to dry with their tongues, unable to open themselves to see our problems. But it's fine for them to pray for us, and we dare not refuse, because remember, we are unholy already. An unknown author wrote, "The hands that help are holier than the lips that pray." Love is the only prayer.

My mind became open, searching every day. I thought about my family and how lucky we really were. We were never faced with many crises; I don't mean "problems"; I mean "crises," the problems that the doctors do not have answers for, ones that the rehab team cannot cure, and ones that keep us up all night only to discover there is still no answer in the morning.

I thought of all the families I knew that went through crises and no amount of money or love could help them. Joan, a family friend I met a few years ago, kept complaining about back pain that hurt her so much that she was unable to take care of her son most of the time. Sometimes, she couldn't get out of bed.

A few months later, I learned that Joan had cancer. She died a few months afterward at age thirty-five. Her mother said the worst thing was seeing her daughter in her last days. That was the second child she was burying. No amount of love or money could have saved Joan's life.

My friend, Jackie, lost her sister to cancer when she was just over forty. She came from Jamaica to visit, and when Jackie went to pick her up at the airport, she fainted when she saw how much her sister had deteriorated. They spent all the money they could on her and gave her all the love and attention she needed but still could not save her life.

I have seen so many people faced with crises they had no control over like motor vehicle accidents claiming the lives of children and parents having to bury them. Children are born with challenging health issues that parents have to deal with. I said to my mother, "God does not love you more than he loves those other parents. But you are luckier than the other parents because you were given a problem that needed only love to cure. You failed; you failed me, not God, but you."

A person can't get wet from the word "water" or be filled by the word "food." Many times, we see food advertisements, and we salivate. But we are not filled. Similarly, the word "love" does not fill or satisfy us. It is the substance of love that satisfies and fills us. I remember as a little girl, my friend, Shernette, and I read fashion magazines and wished we could touch the outfits and make them come alive so we could wear them. They never did, of course. What we saw on those pages only represented the substances.

Love is a substance, something tangible, not just a word on a page. It has to be exercised to be alive. It is an action; it does not exist unless it can be manifested. We have to be able to act out love over and over again to keep it alive. If we muzzle love, it disappears. Unfortunately, we tend to believe love is so natural that it does not need work. Sorry, it needs a lot.

It is love that makes the world go round.

Chapter 7 ❦

Crossing the Line

One day, I received a call from one of my cousins who said he had spoken to Rocky. He said Rocky told him that he wanted to see to it that I was deported back to Jamaica and that Ian took the children from me. My cousin replied, "She is your sister; you both have the same mother and the same father. You might not remember, but you came out of the same belly. So why are you trying to hurt her at a time like this when she is going through so much? Dawn is here, and you are not behaving this way to her. Is she more a sister to you than Lisa?"

To this, my brother answered, "I want her to be here, but I do not want Lisa to be here. She is going to be destroyed. I am going help Ian to destroy her. You will see."

My cousin, shouting curse words at him, said, "Boy, I had no idea that you were so wicked. What could your little sister have done to you to make you hate her so?"

I hung up the phone, and I said over and over again in astounded shock, "They hate me; they hate me; they really, really hate me." I slumped to the floor with a blank stare on my face, because I couldn't believe what I had just heard. I started thinking back on all the fights we had when we were younger.

I knew they were wrong. I knew they were a bit out of place, but honestly, I did not know all those fights could turn into hate.

I started thinking, and a light bulb went off in my head. I said, "I do not hate them." I really thought about it and said, "I cannot hate them." I said, "I will have to learn to hate them; I have to practice to hate them. I have a choice. I will not hate them. Hate is not a good thing; in fact, it is very, very bad. I am sure they did not always hate me, but they have crossed a line." I knew then that there really was a thin line between love and hate.

Love and hate are the two emotions that rule the universe, and there really is a thin line between them. They are both very strong, and the more we exercise them, the stronger they become. Before long, they start to feel comfortable. When I was a little girl, my father used to work construction close to the volatile areas in Kingston. He said that whenever they had a deadline to meet, they would work late in the evenings, sleep at the building site, and wake up early the next morning for work.

He said gunmen would actually talk with the construction crew in the evenings. One evening, as one of them told the story of his killings, he said the first time he killed somebody was so hard for him that he had nightmares about it. Every time he tried to eat, he would see the face of the person and get sick to his stomach. He said when he killed a second person, the feeling was not as bad as the first time. Then he killed again, and it became second nature, because he experienced no ill feelings. He had crossed the line to become a heartless killer, but for him, there was no going back.

Psychologist Erich Fromm wrote, "Every evil act tends to harden a man's heart, that is, to deaden it. Every good deed tends to soften it, to make it more alive. The more a man's heart hardens, the less freedom he has to change, the more he is determined by previous actions. But there comes a point when a man's heart has become so hardened and so deadened that he has lost the possibility of freedom."

I realized long ago that Rocky had developed my father's aggressive personality. They both thought they were right about everything they did and that opposition to their points of view should be condemned. I never paid much attention until Rocky started to declare that he hated my grandmother.

At this point, he had gone too far, and I thought my parents would let Rocky know that it was wrong. They didn't.

Nobody said anything about it. Rather, it became a hide-and-seek situation where everyone would avoid confronting him. For the first time, I started to compare my two grandmothers. The grandmother that he hated was the sweetest old lady. Of course, she had made inappropriate comments and done inappropriate acts, but haven't we all? Hate was much too strong an emotion for someone to bear towards a person who had made these simple mistakes.

My other grandmother, however, was not sociable at all. When friends visited the house, she locked herself in her room until they left. But that was the way she was; I didn't need to hate her because of that.

The hate that Rocky was carrying concerned me so much that one day, I discussed it with my father, because it was his mother that Rocky hated. I asked him why he thought Rocky hated her so much. I wondered if something had happened that I wasn't aware of. My father said that nothing had happened that he knew about, but the whole thing started over a comment that my grandmother made that she did not want anyone in her family to marry into another family, which made no sense to me. I had hoped that my father would address the problem with Rocky, but he never did, and Rocky became more critical of not just my grandmother but almost everyone else.

Rocky and his wife moved to the United States, and we lost contact for a while. But he returned to Jamaica on visits. One day, John, a friend of ours, allegedly died of AIDS. Rocky and I were driving one day, and he said, "Hey, Lisa, I heard that John died of AIDS, and the family is trying to hide it."

"Oh yes, I heard that, too," I responded.

"I am going to ask them about it," he said.

I said, "Boy, you must be mad. You think AIDS is something people just go to the store and buy? It can happen to innocent people. If it is true, we don't know how he got it. Just let them bury their brother with some dignity."

I was really shocked by Rocky's reaction. We have all sinned and come short of the glory of God. Sin may have caused him to die of AIDS, but it is not our place to condemn someone even when he has suffered the ultimate punishment of death. All of us are guilty of participating in gossip, but like anything else, there is that line, that point when we have gone too far, and at that point, it becomes toxic and scary.

On the front page of the *Ocala Star Banner* recently was the story of Zacarias Moussaoui, the alleged hijacker who was supposed to fly the plane into the White House on September 11, 2001. As he faced the families in court, who told the jury how profound the attack had been on their lives, he said, "I found it disgusting that some people will come here to share their grief. Americans should know that grief is precisely what I and fellow fighters in Al Qaeda want to achieve. We want to inflict pain on your country."

When the prosecution asked him about an account of a witness who crawled to safety from a Pentagon corridor demolished on 9/11, Moussaoui replied, "I was sorry that he survived." Zacarias Moussaoui had crossed the line. There was no love inside him; he cannot see and feel anything but hate.

He can't and won't understand the pain and grief of the relatives of those who died on 9/11 because it takes a soft heart to understand grief. His heart is hard and dead. He made those comments while his defense team was pleading for his life, but a person who has reached the point of no return is really dead. He lives only in body, because it impossible to live without love.

This is why we need to fill our hearts with love, because a heart filled with love knows its boundaries and will not drift across the line to hate. The love in our hearts gives a person character, the ability to stand and refuse to pass that point. Remember the saying, "If we don't stand up for what is right, we will fall for anything." It is at the line that we stand firm and refuse to cross over.

Over the years, I have sat my mother down on numerous occasions and explained how I was affected by the beatings, the arguments, and the ultimate rift between my siblings and me. Since she did not respond to the letter I wrote to her when I was a teenager, I assumed she didn't understand what I was going through. My mind went through every moment of my childhood with a fine-toothed comb to try to identify any possibility that she knew that I could have ever been in danger.

The only thing I could come up with was when she visited her mother in Canada for three weeks. While she was gone, she took me to Portland to stay with her relatives. At that time, I was twelve, Grace was twenty-one, Rocky was nineteen, and Dawn was eighteen. My father was always home.

For me, that was an indication that she thought I was in danger, because she took me to someone else's home instead of leaving me in her own and taking the chance that violence could break out. My brother and sisters found the whole thing funny and said, "If Mama didn't take you away to Portland when she wasn't here, we would beat you every day." After that, I started staying away on my own.

When I moved away to New York and my brother tried to set Ian up to destroy me, I called my mother one day crying, screaming in frustration, "I have sat you down so many times over the years and told you what my siblings were doing was wrong, and you ignored me the whole time! You see now what I have been trying to tell you about? You are all going to kill me! When I am going through the worst time of my life, how could you all try to destroy me? If all you can do for me is to destroy my life, it is best for you to stay away from me!"

My parents didn't call me for six months and told people that I told them not to call me, without ever bothering to explain the rest of the conversation. All that concerned my mother was the fact that I told her not to call; any of the anguish I was going through didn't matter. I was having a crisis, and she was only concerned with herself.

I called her six months later, and we started speaking again. I asked her why during all these years, she never took any action on the letter I wrote her or responded to all those times I talked to her about the same issues that were in the letter. She said she kept the letter a secret, because she knew that my siblings would hurt me more if they knew about it.

She missed the whole point of the letter—they were supposed to know about it! She was supposed to sit them down and talk to them about all the violence and the beatings. But as long as there were no broken bones and everyone thought we were the perfect family, the fact that my siblings were beating me didn't matter.

The more she told herself that she did not need to intervene, the more that decision seemed right to her. The more she ignored the beatings and realized that I was trying to work out my own situation, the more she looked the other way.

She said she kept the letter for years, and when we all left home, she threw it away. I wonder what she was keeping it for.

where there is hatred let me sow love ...

prayer of St. Francis

Chapter 8 ❦

The Power of Hate

On September 11, 2001, I was about to grab my keys and head for my car to leave for work when I heard my mother shout, "Oh my God! Lisa, come here! Come look at this!" So I dashed to the living room where she was calling from and saw her standing in front of the television staring at the screen. I was trying to figure out what had alarmed her like that, and there it was—the report of the first plane hitting the World Trade Center. Even though I was late for work that day, I had to take a seat and watch the smoke coming from the twin towers. Many different emotions came through me.

I had made my first visit to Manhattan that summer to see the World Trade Center. My cousins Rickey and Chi-Chi worked near the building. After I saw the TV broadcast, I felt tears running down my face as I thought about them and everybody else in danger.

I grabbed my keys and my handbag and headed to my car. The cheap radio in my car only played R.J.R., and at 9 a.m., it automatically switched to BBC. I was listening to the announcer when he said the other tower had just been hit by another plane. At this point, I thought, "This is not an accident; this must the act of terrorists." The tears started coming faster, and I realized for the first time that hate is a very powerful emotion. The day was very still, as my coworkers at the health center were filled with sorrow and grief for their relatives in New York. It seemed even the animals knew that something was wrong. September 11, 2001, was the first time ever that I knew the power of hate.

I had heard the word "hate" over and over again but never came in contact with the real substance of its fruits. I knew it was a bad thing because I remember Dawn telling me that she hated me, and I told my cousin Nicole that I hated her. But as soon as the words came out of my mouth, I said to myself, "It is not the truth, and I will not say it again." On one occasion, Rocky told me he hated me, and I said to him, "If you say that to me again one more time, I am going to believe you." He said it again one more time jokingly.

People who harbor hate don't have a certain look or come from a specific place. They are not on drugs or on death row. They are walking among you, in suits, preaching, teaching, in the boardrooms, and in high-powered jobs. They earn degrees, live respectful lives, and live in good families, so never assume that people are not capable of hate just because they look or dress a certain way.

One of the chief hijackers, Mohammad Otto, had two master's degrees from one of the most prestigious universities in Europe. Surely, he may have learned something about human love and affection, but hate had already taken over his heart, and he had reached the point of no return. He was tall, dark, and handsome, bright and unassuming, yet he was consumed with hate. He had a mission to do in honor of hate, and it had to be calculated right down to the last minute detail.

Hate is strong enough that the hijackers were willing to give their lives for it and take the lives of innocent people who didn't even know them. Hate was so overwhelming that they would go to any length to nurture it and act it out. Nearly 3,000 people died in that attack—mothers, wives, husbands, and fathers—people whose only crime was being in the wrong place at the wrong time.

Someone once said hate is like cancer. It takes over a person one cell at a time. Like cancer, when hate gets into the system, it spreads, moving from the source that caused the hate in the first place throughout the body for a more generalized effect. If you hate one person, you will hate two. The more persistent hate becomes, the less chance it has to free itself from the destruction of its fruit.

Hate never seeks to build; it is only concerned with destroying. It does not foster peace; it only sets itself on creating war. Hate can't use reasoning; it sets itself on doom and gloom. It does not examine other possibilities; it is only fixed on destruction. Hate kills; it does not create. Hate does not just go away; it may lay dormant. It springs on its prey like a vulture; it is fed, and again, it is strengthened. Hate does not give the benefit of the doubt; rationale, care, or concern. It is for this reason that we should never allow ourselves to be so upset as to go to the extent of hating others. Most of us at some point have been so badly hurt that we would like the people who hurt us to feel how much we hurt by seeing them hurt, but we need to hold the love that is inside us so tightly that love will fill us instead of anger.

Rocky started hating my grandmother, and that hate later spread to the whole family. Love did not exist in his heart enough to kill the feelings of hate that emerged, and he let hate control him. Isaac Newton's first law of motion states that "Every object persists in its state of rest or uniform motion in a straight line unless it is compelled to change that state by force impressed on it." If my parents had intervened at the point Rocky started hating, he might not have continued on the path of hate. Instead, they avoided the confrontation, thus allowing the hate that was born in him to grow, spread, flourish, and strengthen as it grew, giving him less opportunity to reason.

Rocky developed a tremendous hatred for me, for reasons I never understood. Like I mentioned before, I was very concerned with the fact that he hated my grandmother so much. When my grandmother died, I called him and asked if he was coming to pay his respects. He beat around the bush for a while about not having any money to make the trip to Jamaica. I said, "Not many people have spare money lying around, but when situations like this happen, they find a way."

"Okay, listen," he replied, "I am not coming to the funeral because I hate her so much." I had never heard him use these actual words before. It really pierced my heart so much I stopped talking. He started laughing and said,

"Yes, now you heard it right, so eat your heart out." I had nothing left to say; there was nothing to add to such a compelling statement.

We never spoke after that; however, the following summer, I was going to New York, and my mother told me to visit him if I could before I left. I called him that evening. His wife answered the phone, and I started joking around a little, telling her that I was coming to see them in Atlanta next week. "So, who is coming to pick me up?" I jested. I realized that she did not find my jokes amusing, so I said, "Well, I am going to New York next week, but can Rocky come and get me?"

"That will never happen," she responded.

"Tell him to call me," I replied.

Rocky lives in Atlanta, Georgia, drives a trailer truck, and travels all over the United States. My father went to New York once, and Rocky took a load in to New York and picked up my father and brought him to Atlanta with another load. Then, he brought another load to Atlanta and picked up another when he was ready to go back to New York. So I thought this is why my mother wanted me to try to catch him one of his trips into New York. I was in New York for three weeks, but he never called.

The Sunday before I returned to Jamaica, my sister called and asked me if I called Rocky. I said to her, "Honestly, I called him before I came here, and he did not return my call." I told her what his wife said, and a few hours later, his wife called to start an argument with me, asking why I called my sister and told her what she said, if I thought Rocky could beat her. Even though she was carrying on and on, I couldn't understand what she was screaming about, since it was over something that she said.

I didn't speak to Rocky for a year. The next time I went to New York, I asked my cousin to call Rocky for me, which he did. He talked to him for a bit and then said, "Lisa is here, and she wants to talk to you."

But I heard him reply, "I don't want to talk to her."

I took the phone out of my cousin's hand and said, "Why don't you want to talk to me?" After a long pause, while I waited for his answer, I spoke again. "Well, I am in New York, and I'm just calling to say hello."

He said, "Well...hello." And after another long pause, I gave my cousin the phone.

I sat in the apartment for awhile, then got up and walked around thinking. Then I went back to the kitchen where my cousin was still talking to Rocky. I took the phone from him again and said to Rocky, "What is this? What is really going on?"

He replied, "You are acting as if you don't know." I was at a loss for words; I had no idea what he was talking about.

I said, "Honestly, people do things to others and are not aware of the effect they have, but if you tell me what the problem is, then I can understand."

"Well," he replied, "you came to New York last year, and you did not call me, but now you come and call me. What you calling me for, eh? What you calling me for?"

Speaking slowly and making sure I chose the right words, since I realized I was now at war, I responded, "Well, I called you before I came, and you did not return my call."

He began again, "Well, I called all over the place for you. Ask Sonia; ask Dawn and Grace; I called before you left Jamaica, all over the place to look for you."

I replied, "It's a little odd that everybody else who called me got me. I wonder why you called all these people looking for me, and no one bothered to give me the message. I left the message with your wife that I was coming to New York. Why didn't you call me here?"

"How am I supposed to know where you are?" he asked. "You have so many aunts and uncles in New York. How am I supposed to know where you are?"

I answered, "If you had asked any of those people you said you called, they would have told you because they all knew where I went."

He continued to say that his problem with me was that I did not call him on my visit to New York. Ironically, that same week, when he had no idea where I was, his wife found me to begin an argument.

As Rocky continued raving, I said, "Where is this going to end? Life is too short to be going on and on like this. There must be a way to reach an understanding rather than always going on like this. We need to stop."

"I do not need to hear this from the likes of you!" he yelled.

"Well, there seems to be no end to this," I concluded.

We hung up.

Months later, I left Ian for New York. Four days after I left, Rocky called to ask me for Ian's number. Even though this time, I was not staying with the uncle I always stayed with when I came to New York, Rocky somehow found me after only four days—not three weeks. I gave him the number because even though I was fully aware that we were not on the best of terms, never in a million years did I think it was so bad that he would try to hurt me. He called Ian, told him where I was, and told him to call the police on me. We do not know the effects of hate unless we have hated.

The measure of a man is not where he stands in moment of comfort and convenience, but where he stands in time of challenge and controversy ...

Martin Luther King

Chapter 9 ❦

True Colors

After living with Ian and realizing that he was cheating on me, I decided to leave him. We had two children together, and we owned a house, so leaving was not as easy as packing up and moving out. I left after more than two years of negotiation to try to save our relationship. I told him that there was no way I could force him to stay in a relationship he no longer wanted to be in. I said it would not do us any good if I wanted the relationship 100 percent if he didn't want it just as much. Then, I pointed out that we needed to make a decision in the best interest of the children. I assured him that no matter what happened to us, I would never keep the children from him.

First, I asked him to move out and see the children on weekends. But he told me that he'd prefer to burn the house down before he moved out. When I realized he was steadfast in his intent, I had a meeting with a few of my friends to organize an intervention. I told them that the purpose for this action was not to expose our problems but to allow Ian to realize that this relationship was not just about him. Our children deserved to be comfortable in their own home. All I was asking was that he move out, go on with his own life, and allow the children to ease into the situation of not having their parents together. I didn't want the children to not have their family at all and have to move from the only house they know.

The children felt a sense of belonging. They had their own room and their own beds. They knew this was their home. Whenever they went to their grandparents' house and I called them, they always said, "Mommy, we are ready to come home now." At the time of the intervention, my daughter was two years old and my son was only a year old. We had already developed our own concepts about life, and we were mature and set in our ways. However we handled this, it would affect how the children developed their own perceptions about their lives. So, the aim was to minimize the trauma to the children.

The meeting was tense with Ian insisting he was not going to move out. That same year, I started college full time, and Ian did not make an effort to change his ways. I went through the first year of school being very depressed. At the end of the academic year, I thought I would attend summer classes so I could finish college at least one semester early. I would then be able to move out on my own since it was too much for me to take care of the children, go to school full time, and move out. The situation at home grew worse by the day. During my summer classes, I made the decision to leave right then because the living situation was getting progressively worse.

Two particular incidents caused me to make the decision to leave. They might seem insignificant, but the "little things" are what broke me. My daughter had an ear infection and was running a fever for three days. The nurse practitioner at the clinic where I worked examined her and gave me some medication for her. I called Ian and told him that Afreka had an ear infection. I then gave her the medication and went to school. Ian left work at 4:30 p.m., so I thought he would be home by the time I arrived at school. When I pulled into the driveway that evening, I realized that Ian did not come home. I didn't think I had to tell him he needed to be home because his child was ill. I felt like a single mother. If I had not been living with their father, I would have made arrangements without considering him. But I figured Ian would put off whatever he had planned that night since his daughter was ill.

My summer classes ran Monday, Tuesday, and Thursday evenings for eight consecutive weeks. On Mondays, I had classes from 7 p.m. to 9 p.m. As I sat outside waiting to go to class one Monday evening, Ian called to tell me that he was unable to come home. I replied, "But you know that my classes don't end until 9 p.m., and it takes me more than an hour to get home. Tracey has been there since 8 this morning, and I can't ask her to stay until 10:30."

He said, "I already called Tracey and told her that I will not be home and that she should stay until you come home."

As soon as I hung up the phone, Tracey called me to say I should pick up the children at her house when I got home. I really was a single mother at this point, and domestic life, school, and the children were just too much for me to handle alone. I knew I had to leave. It was bad enough that he was cheating on me, but he could have at least shown a little care for his children and a little respect for me. I went to school three nights a week; he could at least choose the nights that I did not go to school to go about his business and be there when I couldn't.

More than three years went by, and my problems with Ian continued to get worse. It wasn't going to do me any good to remain at home and pretend that everything was fine. I had to get out, so I sold my car, took the money that I had saved to pay my college tuition, and left with just two suitcases and my children. I was as depressed as I could ever be. This was the perfect time for my family members to show their true colors, and they did.

Have you ever heard the story of the donkey? Once up on a time, a man had a donkey that fell into a well. He called his neighbors and friends and asked them, "What shall we do with this donkey? It has fallen so deep into the well, so how can we help it?"

One wise, lazy person answered, "Since it has fallen into the well, it will be easer for us to bury it." So they gathered together friends, families, and neighbors and proceeded to bury the donkey. The well was so deep that they had to get a truckload of dirt for the burial. The dirt came and everyone got to work with their shovels, pickaxes, and buckets, and they started packing in the dirt.

With every shovel of dirt that was thrown on the donkey's back, he shook it off, and it fell to his feet. Soon, he was standing on the dirt. The heaps of dirt came faster and faster, harder and harder, and in order to survive, the donkey had no choice but to shake it off. There were times when he became overwhelmed by the constant heaps of dirt, times when it seemed as if he could not shake it off enough, but he only had to move and the dirt would fall to his feet. He kept getting higher and higher with each mound of dirt that was meant to bury him. He got weak sometimes because the dirt had sharp rocks in it that cut his back, but he kept shaking it off. He continued to shake it off until the dirt around him was so high that he could just walk right out of the well. When he got out of the well and saw all the people he had known who had dumped dirt on him, he looked at them very differently. He was wounded, lame, tired, and bruised all over. All he could do was rest awhile and try to recover alone in the darkest night, cold and exhausted.

I have lived the experience of that fallen donkey. I have been told that of all human crises, the breakup of a relationship ranks second to the highest in terms of the stress it has on an individual, second only to death of a loved one. Some believe the two should be ranked equally, since losing a relationship is often accompanied by rejection, betrayal, and deceit.

I never in my wildest dreams thought that my own family would have reacted the way they did to the decision I made to move out. In a crisis like this, we need the comfort and support of our families. Not getting the support from them was bad enough, but to go a step further and turn on me and side with Ian was more than I could take. My brother and sisters told Ian my every move and that he shouldn't worry because my money would eventually run out, and I would then have to send the children to him.

I knew we weren't close, but I had no idea that level of hate existed between us. Grace gave me the first taste of it. Early in the summer that I left Jamaica, Dawn called to borrow some money. I loaned it to her because she still had time to repay me before I returned to school in September. She said she would let Grace give it back to me. By the time I was ready to go back to school, I told Grace that she could put the money back in my account.

A few weeks went by, and it was still not in my account, so I gave Grace a specific date to put it in. On Monday of that week, I told her to leave it in my account by Wednesday. On Tuesday morning of the following week, I called my supervisor to tell her I would be late for work because I had some personal business to take care of. I went to the bank to join the line. Can you imagine my surprise and anger when I found out that the money was not in the bank?

I took a seat in the bank for a while to compose myself. Then I called Grace and asked, "How could I ask you to put my money in the bank for a week now, and I am here at the bank, and it is still not in my account? I had to take time off from work, and the money is still not in my account! I am really upset!"

She replied, "Give me the account number."

"I can't believe you don't even have the account number that I gave you weeks ago," I replied. "If you realized you lost it, you should have called me so I could give it to you again."

It seemed as if she had no intention of putting my money in my account. So I gave her the account number and went back to work. She called me at work and said the money was in my account, and then she cussed me out, telling me that I always thought I was better and brighter than everybody else. At this point, she knew I was leaving Ian in a few days and that I was depressed already.

She sounded as if she was having fun. I said, "Oh, so this is what the fighting has always been about." I could not believe that at the worst time of my life, my sister was heaping all of this on me. To make matters worse, she seemed to have thought it all out in vivid detail. I never heard any of this when my life was progressing well, and she did not even take the time to say she sympathized with what I was going through.

I went to New York that week and called Dawn. She asked, "So what are you calling me for now?"

I said, "What do you mean? I did not call you when I was in Jamaica? As far as I can remember, I was the one who called you last and emailed you last." She did not reply. After a long pause, I gave my cousin the phone.

Four days after I arrived in New York, Rocky called me to ask me for Ian's number. He then called him right away to tell him where I was and that I did not have my son with me. Remember when I came to New York months before he claimed he did not know where I was? Remember when he said he was calling all over the place for me and could not find me for weeks? Yet four days after I arrived this time, he found me. And further, this was only time I stayed with my aunt. The other times, I stayed with my uncle.

Before I left Jamaica, I had planned to take both my children with me, but no one was willing to accommodate me with both babies. So at the last minute, I had to leave my son with plans to get him as soon as I got situated. I was extremely shocked to find out that my family was out to destroy me in my time of crisis. And no one would benefit from it, not even Ian. In fact, Rocky encouraged him to go to the police and let them find me and my children. Ian actually took days off from work to take the police to the clinic to question my coworkers about me as if I were a criminal. People who saw Ian during that time said he looked like a madman.

The stress really started to get to me. One evening, when I was at the restaurant where I worked, I suddenly became very weak. So I sat down, rubbed my hand over the back of my head, and felt several big bumps. They were stiff and I thought I was going to die, because they felt as if they had been sitting on my veins and they would burst any minute. A few days after, my head oozed with puss and my skin broke out in hives. Then I went to Kings County Hospital. When the doctor examined me, he had no idea what the lumps were. So, while I sat there with my top off, he called all the doctors into the emergency room to show them my skin. They scheduled me for the skin clinic and gave me a prescription for an antibiotic. My doctor gave me a printout of the possible causes for the skin condition, which turned out to be "extreme stress." That's when I really knew the stress had taken its toll on me.

In every person from the cradle to the grave
there is a deep craving to be appreciated.

Chapter 10 ❦

We Are More Alike Than We Think

For summer holidays, I always visited my uncle's house. When life was great, I was very welcome. I had already completed one full year at college and was planning to transfer to a New York university when I left Ian. I called my uncle to ask whether the children and I could stay with him in the meantime. After a long pause, I told him I knew it was a lot to ask and I knew he was coming to Jamaica in two weeks, so we could talk about it when he arrived. He agreed.

While he was in Jamaica, he gave me the cold shoulder his entire visit. All of my relatives were there for a family reunion in Hayes and a Friday evening devotion. I tried to talk to my uncle, but as soon as I tried to approach him, he made a beeline for my cousin. I got the message.

I went to another uncle, and even before I finished telling him what I needed, he agreed that I could stay at his home. He and his family came to my house to work out the final details.

He told me about the preschool near his house and that he would tell me more about it when he checked out the details.

Unfortunately, later, he called to tell me that his son was returning from another state, so he was unable to accommodate me after all. So I asked my cousin, who said she would work something out. She told her mother, my aunt, and asked me if it was possible to come without the children. She knew it would be really hard on me and the children to be separated, so she told me to really think about it. Since I was running out of time, I had no choice but to leave one of my children, so I left my son.

When I arrived in New York, I discovered so much happening behind my back. I found it strange the way my uncle carried on, but I still called him when he returned to find out if he reached home safely. Upon my arrival in New York, I called my uncle Glen to ask him to open a bank account for me, which he did. Tension built between Rocky and Ian, and I began to realize that much more was happening than I thought. I called my uncle one day and said to him, "Tell me something, what is your take on me leaving my children the way I did and coming to New York?"

"Why are you asking me?" he responded. "That is no business of mine."

I said, "No, but I came here in my situation, and you never even asked me whether I'm fine or offered to help in any way."

"What do you want me to do, eh?" he replied. "What do you want me to do?"

I didn't say anything because there was so much that he could do. About a week later, I went to my family's bi-monthly meeting and told them how disappointed I was with them. Then I learned that before I arrived in New York, the family met and voted that no one should help me. Many things then started to make sense.

So, everybody was giving me excuses as to why they couldn't help me, when all the while, there was a vote governing their decisions. I couldn't understand that at all. I left Ian because I could no longer cope with his affairs, and my own family voted against me. I thought about the possible reasons for their decision. My aunt, who was hosting the meeting, had to leave her husband for the same reasons that I left Ian. I looked around the room and saw only one uncle who had not been through a separation or divorce.

My uncle Glen was my greatest surprise, not only because he was the one I was closest to, but he also had been through the same situation that I was going through. He was living with his children's mother, Sandie, and they had two children almost the same ages as mine—one boy and one girl, same as mine. When they separated, no one condemned him. Instead, the family assisted him with his children so he could get on with his life. I still remember sitting at church one night when a family member told my mother that Sandie had left, and Glen was alone with the children.

After church that night, my mother and I went to see Glen, and the children were fast asleep when we arrived. My mother talked with him and told him it was too late to take the children with us that evening. So, the following day, my mother sent me for the boy and another uncle took the girl. My uncle got the help and support he needed to pick up the pieces and start over again. He went to his job every day as a bus driver without worrying how his children were being cared for.

It made a big difference for Glen that he had someone to help him with his children. Two years after his son came to live with us, his daughter came also. A year later, he got married and later had a son from that marriage; that son came to live with us, too, when my uncle and his wife moved to the United States. The children lived with us another four years afterward. They lived with us for about ten years altogether.

The arrangement worked so well that they had the chance to go to the United States and work without having their children to worry about. By the time they took the children to the United States, they had already bought a house.

While the children were living with us, my uncle gave me the responsibility to teach them. I felt important, and I put my whole self into it as if it were my job. My uncle and his wife had sent a set of Dr. Seuss books, and my little cousins could read every one. I felt so proud when anyone came to the house; I would just show off my work by calling my cousins and letting them read to everyone.

After they went to live with their parents in the United States, my cousin Nichole came back to visit us for the summer. My uncle told me that I was responsible for my cousin, so I stood by my responsibility.

My aunt, who was the chairperson of the family meeting I attended, left her daughter for a while until she got situated. Another aunt who was at the meeting was so stressed when she had her daughter that she actually thought of leaving her in the hospital. With the help of her family, however, she survived the stress. But now that they had managed to pass that stage, they did not remember a time when they were not perfect.

When I spoke to Rocky to find out why he was so angry with me, his arguments were incredibly confusing. He talked about me seeing a Rasta man after I was brought up in a Christian family. He said I had no right to build a house with a man I wasn't married to. So I asked, "If we were living at my parents' house, wouldn't you ask us why we were there and not buying our own home since we are working?"

My getting involved with a man who was not in the church was no longer an issue. But I asked him, "Do you know that more than half of all marriages end in divorce? I am sure that most people who enter into a marriage do so with high hopes. I am sure you have seen breakups even in the church." He could not think of anybody who joined together in a Godly union and ended up in a careless situation like mine. After we argued back and forth, I hung up the phone. Rocky somehow overlooked the fact that his mother-in-law was married to one of the leaders in our church, and they had a very messy divorce.

When we are ready to judge and condemn others, our outlook can change drastically. If we realize that the people we are trying to condemn made similar mistakes to ours, we would not be so eager to crucify them. The Bible gives an example of a woman who was caught in the act of adultery. People gathered around her to stone her after they complained to Jesus about her sinful act. Jesus replied, "If any one of you is without sin, let him be the first to throw a stone at her" (John 8:7). They all put away their stones and went their own way. When Jesus looked around, he saw the woman all by herself and asked where all of her accusers went.

Jesus did not actually tell the crowd they could not stone the woman; he simply instructed them how to. If we take time to see how similar our situations are to others, the world would be a better place.

When I cried over my situation, Rocky told me about the starving children in Africa who have no food to eat and that I was the one acting as if I was going to die. He told me to get over it, get a life, and move on. He shouted it as if he were preaching it from the pulpit. My good friend, T.D. Jakes, said, "We are living in a get-over-it generation. People think they have a right to harm others as long as we can tell them to get over it, get a life, and move on."

If I could stop one heart break, I will not livei in vain.

Chapter 11 ❦

My Knight in Shining Armor

M any times, when we see a tragic situation in the news, we think, "Oh, that only happens to other people." One day, when I was on maternity leave with my daughter, I happened to be watching the news. The news reported that a man in Mandiville gave his wife and daughter poison to drink and then killed himself. The couple were college graduates in their thirties. I thought to myself, "What could have gone so wrong that he felt he had to poison someone he once loved and his own daughter?" Could he not find anyone to help him resolve the problems with his wife?

A dentist in Texas ran her husband over with her car, moving the car back and forth until he was dead because he was cheating on her. The report on the incident said she found notes he had written comparing her to the other woman he was seeing. So she snapped and ran him over.

Scott Peterson killed his pregnant wife, Lacy, because he was cheating on her and he must have been so deep into the other relationship that he wanted to get rid of his wife. Was there no other way to deal with this than to resort to violence? Couldn't he leave her and go to the other woman whom he obviously loved more? One news reporter commented that any man can cheat, but it takes a smart man to stop.

The absence of love is not necessarily hate, but the fruit of love is not just affection but also rational thinking and seeing clearly when faced with a critical decision. Ultimate love begins with oneself; you cannot give adequately what you do not possess abundantly in yourself. This next quote is from one of my social work classes:

> I love myself so much,
> so I love you so much,
> so you love you so much,
> so you can start loving me.

The opposite of love can sometimes be fear instead of hate. Scott Peterson may not have hated his wife when he murdered her, but he was certainly not centered by love. So while he strayed from love and stood on the thin line, he developed fear. He couldn't admit to the lies he was telling the other woman or leave his wife. Instead, he let fear dictate his choice and didn't even make the easier one, because that would have been to leave his wife and son alive and avoid prison. He not only ended the life of his wife and son, he also destroyed himself in the process. It is impossible to destroy someone else without destroying a little bit of yourself.

While I went through the depression from Ian's lying and cheating and the demands of my babies, I thought to myself, "These things don't just happen to other people; right now, it is happening to me." I wanted it to end so badly that I thought about killing both Ian and myself. I thought of my children, but I wanted to leave them out of it. Then I thought, "How could I leave them out of it if they grow up without their mother and learned that she took her own life?" If I killed their father, I would be in prison and he would be dead, so my children would have neither of us. I knew I would never get a hit man. I wanted to do it myself because the pain was too much, and I wouldn't give another person the pleasure of killing him. Even though good reasoning won that battle, the situation was consistent, and I wanted to be numb even for a while.

One day at work, the situation overwhelmed me so much that I thought about taking drugs. I was trying to do my regular end-of-the-month report at the clinic, and I just couldn't do it. So I asked my assistant to do it for me, and I got in my car to go get a fix.

I had no idea where to get drugs because I had never taken drugs before, nor did I know anyone else who had. As I drove, I saw a man whom I thought somehow could give me that information. I pulled over and made up a story about a cousin who was on drugs whom we couldn't find for days. So I asked him to please tell me where to find a place that sells drugs, because I might find him there.

He told me exactly where to get the drugs. I was on my way. I had enough money on me, and I was going to buy twice as much as I needed. As I drove, I saw my girlfriend Sonia who told me to pull over when she saw me. She asked me where I was going, so I told her. But she insisted that she was not about to allow me to take any drugs. She tried incessantly to talk me out of it, but it was not working. So she took my phone and started to call the numbers stored in my phone to tell everyone what I was about to do. She insisted that she was going to change her plans because she was not about to leave until she was sure that I was going home.

Somehow, she convinced me to go home and sleep off the feeling. She said she would cover for me at work. So I headed home, my mind blank as I hit the highway, except for a little voice in my head that said to me, "Each of us has our own space in this world. We must occupy it until the giver of the space says that our time has expired." I made up my mind then that I was never going to allow anyone to ever bring me to the point where I would have to resort to drastic measures that would destroy me.

As home life got progressively worse, I resorted to drinking Jamaican white rum to put me to sleep. After drinking it for two nights, I decided I was not going to allow myself to become a drunkard, so I never did it again.

No matter how strong we are as individuals, we can only stand so much pressure by ourselves. My family was the first source of help I turned to, but all I got from them was judgment and prayer. So I had to search for another source.

I remember reading a story about a little girl who was from a Christian family. One night, after her parents prayed with her, tucked her into bed with her teddy bear, turned off the lights, and put her to sleep, she cried out as her parents left the room. So they rushed back to her room, and the little girl said, "I am scared."

Her mother replied, "But you have your teddy bear, and you know that God is watching over you."

The little girl thought for awhile then said, "Yes, I know that, but I need somebody with skin on."

In my lowest days, I had to stand strong and draw strength from every positive thing around me. I started reading books by T.D. Jakes and watching *The Potter's Touch*. It seemed as if T.D. Jakes was talking to me through those books and that he came on *The Potter's Touch* every day just to talk to me. As I sank lower and lower, he came out of the books and the television and stood over me. One night, after I put the babies to sleep, I went to take a shower, but the moment I took my clothes off and turned on the water, my son started crying. I got out of the shower and stood at the bathroom door trying to decide whether to go out the front door or go pick up my son first and then head for the front door.

As I reached for the door handle, there he was, T. D. Jakes, standing over me big, strong, and serious, saying, "You may die someday on something, but you are not going to die today like this." He shouted, "Push! You don't have time to cry. Push! You don't have time to be suicidal. Push! This is not the time to give up. Push! Because God is about to birth a promise through you. Cry if you must, and groan if you have to, but keep on pushing because God has a promise that if it is to come into this world, it got to pass through you."

That passage is taken from the book *Woman Thou Art Loosed*. I would pick up the book and read just that passage when I was extremely depressed. In fact I underlined it and came to know it by heart, that night it was as if it was not enough for me to recite the passage; T.D. Jakes had to come there in person and refuse to let me go through that door.

I let go of the door handle and went to the room to pick up my son. Then I got back into the shower. As I went to bed that night, I started chanting, "Do, Lord, have mercy on me. Do, Lord, have mercy on me," until I fell asleep.

As I woke up the next morning, I thought for the first time, "How could a man write those words and compare those words to the birth of my son?" I thought it was an interesting analogy and assumed only a woman could have made that comparison.

Crises like those remind me of being in labor. Even though I know the child is inside me, I know it has to come out, and since I have no choice, I just have to endure it until it is born. During the labor, the pain comes and I push. When the pain stops, I stop pushing, and during that time, I know that I am going to make it and I feel hopeful until another wave of pain comes and I have to push again.

I was an awful patient when I was having my son. The pain came, and I screamed at the nurse, "I am going to die! I am going to die! You all know that I am going to die, and you don't even care!" Then the pain stopped, and I started singing, "Call the nurse." Then I started laughing and telling her, "I am going to have this baby; you will see." Then the pain came again, and I cried, screamed, and pushed. Finally, Dakhari came, and I was tired, but the pain completely stopped, and I felt like I could run a marathon.

The comparison made by T. D. Jakes between crises and the birth of a child is unmistakable. There is no other way to get the baby out except to go through the pain. Like the contractions a mother experiences during the birth of her child, sometimes there is a stillness in the middle of the crisis. At that time, we have to gather our strength for when the pain comes.

Harold S. Kushner was another person who was present in my times of crises. After I brought my children to school in New York one morning, I got on the bus and went to Kings Plaza and wandered aimlessly. I went into a bookstore and bought *The Lord is My Shepherd* by Harold S. Kushner. As I read, "Yea, though I walk through the valley of the shadow of death I will fear no evil for thou art with me" became my new chant.

As the pressure mounted, I chanted to put myself to sleep at night. This became my chant the whole time I was in New York. I realized I was in the valley of the shadow of death because the pain was so unbearable I felt like killing myself. On top of that, I thought my own family was killing me. When they turned their backs on me, I went to Florida to stay with a friend. When I got there, I called my uncle who saw me off at the airport to say I had arrived safely. Then he told me that Ian was looking for me.

I realized that my sisters and brother had given him the information on how to get to me so that he could come and take my children. I realized then why so many women stay in a bad relationship instead of leaving; because once you try to leave, you are judged by your own family.

My body could not take it anymore. The Sunday I went to Ocala, Florida, my period ended. When I heard Ian was looking for me, I could no longer cope. I bled so heavily for a week that I couldn't even get out of bed. When I got up to walk, I had to hold on to the wall for support. I couldn't even take care of my children. One evening, my friend's daughter made dinner for my children, and I tried to get to the kitchen to share their dinner. As I grabbed the plates, I started to fall, so I struggled back to my room.

When I got back to bed, I started to chant, "I am in the valley of the shadow of death, and I am scared." I started to pray, but I was sure that God was not hearing me. My body grew weaker and weaker, and, once again, I thought of suicide. I eventually got better physically, but I was still in the valley, way down there, where I had a lot of getting up to do.

By this time, I was sure God had forgotten about me. I stopped praying because it no longer made any sense. I started to gain strength and decided that I was going to take my children and myself safely out of this valley. I changed my chant again. This time, it said, "Yea, though I walk through the valley of the shadow of death, I will fear no evil even if thou are not with me." I chanted, chanted, and chanted some more, but I could not pray.

I could not understand God. I questioned him. I asked him, "Carest thou that I perish? Carest thou not that my children perish?" I needed an answer; this was not what I learned in Sabbath school. I knew there was a God, one who cared for me even though I sinned. I was not as faithful and holy as Job was, but I was his and that was all that mattered. I learned that God was there for me regardless of my sins. Where was the God who was there for me though my sins be as scarlet? Where was the God of mercy? I needed some answers.

I laughed and said to myself, "Okay, God, you are for real. If all those people say you are there and you are merciful and nobody ever said you failed, you are for real. If you work for 99 percent of the people 99 percent of the time, then you pass. In fact, you get an A+. But between you and me, you failed me! You did, but that is fine because I am in the minority. I say you have no right to fail me, and I need some answers."

Render to caesar the things that are caesars
and unto god the things that are god's

Chapter 12 🌱

I Still Believe in God

Reluctantly, I started to read my Bible, but I was still not praying because God and I were not on speaking terms. I read Job, and for the first time, I realized that he and I were a lot alike. I wasn't holy and righteous, but during Job's ordeal, his friends kept accusing him of being a bad person every step of the way and saying he had done things to cause his suffering. I had the same experience. But Job refused to shut up because he was sure he didn't do anything to cause his circumstances. Well, that was me; I refused to shut up.

As I read the book, *When Bad Things Happen to Good People* by Harold S. Kushner, things became clearer to me. In his book, he noted:

> If the Jews had behaved differently, Hitler would not have been driven to murder them. If the young woman had not been so provocatively dressed, the man would not have assaulted her. If people worked harder, they would not be poor. If society did not taunt poor people by advertising things they cannot afford, they would not steal. Blaming the victim is a way of reassuring ourselves that the world is not as bad a place as it may seem, and that there is good reason for people's suffering. It helps fortunate people believe that their good

fortune is deserved, rather than being a matter of luck. It makes everyone feel better except the victim, who now suffers the double abuse of social condemnation on top of his original misfortune.

I realized that God had not failed me; man did. I was not excused from the fresh air, food, and shelter. With all that was going on around me, my children and I were not hospitalized. In fact, we were in fairly good health. I still had good eyesight, which is one of the senses that fills me up. As I flew from Orlando to New York and looked down below, the view filled me with the excitement that it always did when we descended in New York and saw the snow-covered ground for the first time. I was filled with awe.

My mind went back to a classmate of mine who was blind, and she was trying to get her degree in spite of her limitation. I smiled and said, "I can see; I can see." I have a reason to go on. I was on the plane thinking I needed winter clothes for my children and that I would have to get them with the money I earned from my trip to Florida. I left my children with my friend Lorna for the weekend, and when I got home, I discovered that Lorna and her husband had already bought them everything that I was planning to get them and more—new jeans, pants, undershirts, sweaters, scarves, and jackets.

God had not failed me. In fact, he never left me. People failed me. He was still supplying my needs according to his riches in glory. As I read my Bible, I came across Proverbs 18:14 (NIV): "A man's sprit sustains him in sickness, but a crushed spirit who can bear?"

Feeling rejected, judged, abandoned, and accused of things I didn't do was more than I could stand. I prayed, but there seemed to be no answer to my prayers. I believed in prayer all my life and wondered what I was going to teach my children about prayer. I decided I would explain to them that there is a place for prayer and a time for action. There must be some action for which you ask the blessing. If we need a job, we do not sit at home and pray for one. We apply for the job, put on our best suit, act our best in the interview, and pray that God will help us get the job. It's the same when buying a house or a car or taking an exam. We take action and ask God for His blessings on what we have no control over.

There was no lack of prayer in my situation, but there was a total absence of action. I borrowed this poem from *When Bad Things Happen to Good People*:

We cannot merely pray to you, oh God, to end war,
For we know that you have made the world in a way
That man must find his own path to peace
Within himself and with his neighbor.
We cannot merely pray to you, oh God, to end starvation
For you have already given us the resources,
With which to feed the entire world
If we would only use them wisely.
We cannot merely pray to you, Oh God,
To root out prejudice,
For you have already given us eyes,
With which to see the good in all man
If we would only use them rightly.
We cannot merely pray to you, oh God, to end despair,
For you have already given us the power
To clear away slum and give hope,
If we would only use our power justly.
We cannot merely pray to you, oh God, to end disease,
For you have already given us great minds with which
To search out cures and healing,
If we would only use them constructively.
Therefore we pray to you instead, oh God,
For strength, determination, and will power,
To do instead of just to pray
To become instead of merely to wish.

Jack Riemer, Likrat Shabbat

As I went through the sufferings of losing my relationship with Ian and leaving my comfort zone, my secure job, and my education while taking care of my children, there were things I needed from the people closest to me and not just prayer. I needed a shoulder to cry on; help with my children; kind, comforting words; encouragement; affirmation; hope; love; understanding; care; cooperation; and support, all of which are simple pleasures of life, things that didn't need prayer.

Mind you, I'm not saying I didn't need prayer; I am saying prayer alone was not enough. I did not have a terminal disease nor was I on death row, but that was how I felt when my family turned their backs on me. The true test of a person's character is not where he or she stands when times are great and wonderful; how they react when you are at your lowest really says who is on your side and who your friends really are.

As I searched for answers, I found there was not one case where God turned his back on his people without trying his best with us. He embraces the sinful, and for that reason, he left heaven to come to earth to show us how to live. He took on humanity so that we may put on divinity.

As God walked among men, he did not judge; he only loved.

The smallest good deed is better
than the greatest intention.

Chapter 13 🖤

Finally, Brethren

When I was in high school, I was a part of the debating club. I loved it. I remember once we were supposed to debate "Money or education, which is more important?" We had to choose whether to argue for or against that issue by selecting our choice from a bag. In my mind, I believed that education was more important than money, but my team chose "Money is more important." I was so disappointed that I went to my English teacher and told her that I didn't know how my team was going to win the debate because I believed that education was more important than money.

She said to my team, "Go and research the topic as if you believed that money is more important than education." We did just that, and we won the debate. We were on the ball from the main speaker right down to the final arguments. We rebutted every unexpected question that the other team shot at us.

I learned two things from this experience. One is that whatever we get in life is what we have to play. We can't change the person we are or our relatives or their beliefs. We can't change where we are or the family we were born into. We need only to identify what we want out of life and assure ourselves we can get there. The second thing I learned is we will only win if we believe in what we do.

As I spoke to my mother and sister about the problems I was having at home, I sensed their lack of understanding. I said to my sister, "You can only help me if you believe me. It takes no more time to see the good side of life than it takes to see the bad. It is all a matter of choice. We all have good in us, and in every situation, there is good and bad. But it is only with the heart of love that we can see correctly. The most important things are not visible with the eye but rather with a heart that is filled with love."

Every day, we touch people's lives with the things we do. Endeavor to touch them with love. The more we surround ourselves with love, the less effort we need to put into it. Over and over again, the Bible stresses the importance of knowledge and understanding. It emphasizes that in all your getting, get understanding. Only by using knowledge and understanding can we see with a heart of love and when our assistance is required.

A friend of mine was going through a separation, and I thought about how sad she must feel. So, I called and asked her if she wanted to go to a movie. She agreed without hesitation. We drove into Kingston early enough to browse through the mall and buy something. We laughed and talked about everything, even though I had no idea whether she caused the break-up, and frankly, I didn't care—that was not my main focus. When someone loses a relationship for whatever reason, there is tremendous pain. People are nourished and sustained by love and relationships. To lose them is to take away a part of a person.

So often, we are faced with people who need to be replenished from losing a part of themselves when they have gone through losing their loved ones. By the time we stop to figure out whether that person deserves the loss, it may be too late to help them. Edger Watson Howe wrote, "If a friend is in trouble, don't annoy him by asking if there is anything you can do. Think up something appropriate and do it."

When a person is going through problems, people get the most critical. They will connect situations that had nothing to do with the problem to make it seem as if the person deserved the misfortune. Someone once said, "A critical spirit is like poison ivy; it only takes a little contact to spread its poison." Avoid spreading the poison. Stand up and stand out. When the poison is spreading, spread something sweet instead. As I once read, "Reckless words pierce like a sword, but the tongue of a wise brings healing." What will it be for you? Healing or death? Poison often results in death...choose wisely.

I would like to share this story that was emailed to me:

DON'T FOLLOW THE FOLLOWER

Ninety-five percent of people never succeed because they're following the wrong group.

Processionary caterpillars travel in long, undulating lines, one behind the other. Jean Henri Fabre, the French entomologist, once led a group of these caterpillars onto the rim of a large flowerpot so that the leader of the procession found himself nose to tail with the last caterpillar in the procession, forming a circle without end or beginning.

Through sheer force of habit, and of course, instinct, the ring of caterpillars circled the flowerpot for seven days and seven nights, until they died from exhaustion and starvation. An ample supply of food was close at hand and plainly seen, but it was outside of the range of the circle, so the caterpillars continued along the beaten path.

People often behave similarly. Habit patterns and ways of thinking become deeply established, and it seems easier and more comforting to follow them than to cope with change, even when that change may represent freedom, achievement, and success.

If someone shouts "Fire!" people automatically blindly follow the crowd, and many thousands have needlessly died because of it. How many stop to ask themselves: Is this really the best way out of here?

So many people "miss the boat" because it's easier and more comforting to follow—to follow without questioning the qualifications of the people just ahead—than to do some independent thinking and checking.

A hard thing for most people to fully understand is that people in such numbers can be so wrong, like the caterpillars going around and around the edge of the flowerpot with life and food just a short distance away. If most people are living that way, it must be right, they think. But a little checking will reveal that throughout all recorded history, the majority of mankind has an unbroken record of being wrong about most things, especially important things. For a time, we thought the earth was flat, and later, we thought the sun, stars, and planets traveled around the earth. Both ideas are now considered ridiculous, but at the time, they were believed and defended by the vast majority of followers. In the hindsight of history, we must look like those caterpillars blindly following the leader out of habit rather than stepping out of the line to look for the truth.

Many times, the people in the procession believe that they are right because their group is bigger, and people are convinced that the majority has to be right. But it is not always so. My favorite chapter in the Bible, Ephesians 6:10-14 (KJV), gives us the confidence to do the right thing even if we stand alone:

> Finally, be strong in the Lord and in his mighty power. Put on the full armor of God so that you can take your stand against the devil's schemes. For our struggle is not against flesh and blood, but against the rulers, against the authorities, against the powers of this dark world and against the spiritual forces of evil in the heavenly realms. Therefore put on the full armor of God, so that when the day of evil comes, you may be able to stand your ground, and after you have done everything, to stand. Stand firm then, with the belt of truth buckled around your waist, with the breastplate of righteousness in place.

Many times, after we have given our all, we still fail, but it is not at that time that it is over. We can only win if we believe in what we do, and that is when we need the truth to wrap tightly around us, because it is the only thing that can save us when the evil days come. If we look with a heart of love, we will be able to see the truth.

No matter what state or circumstance
you find your self in, give thanks

Chapter 14 ❦

I Am Truly Grateful

I had a lot of fun with my family when life was going well for me. I remember on one of my trips to New York when my life was fine (or at least seemed fine), my uncle and his wife were at the airport waiting for me in eager excitement. When I approached the waiting area, I saw my aunt-in-law screaming my name as soon as she saw me. Then I saw another lady I didn't even know screaming my name. I looked at her quizzically and asked my uncle and his wife, "Who was that?"

They said, "Oh, she is just some lady who was waiting on Air Jamaica with us."

My uncle took me everywhere he went, and another uncle gave me money for shopping. I spent time with my aunts, and those days were a lot of fun; I am truly grateful.

I am grateful for Dawn who took care of my children many times and kept my daughter Afreka when I was in the hospital having my son. She also allowed me to stay at her house when I had late classes and helped me to type my course papers. I am grateful to my parents who took my children whenever I had exams and everyone else who ever gave me any form of help. I want to take this opportunity to thank you.

And for those people who were there for me at my lowest, stand up and take a bow—my coworkers at the York Town health center, Sally and Marline, who took my son away from me before he was six months when I was in the worst of my depression and allowed me to sleep through the weekends and take care of my daughter. I want to thank you, too.

The night before I left Jamaica, they tried to trick me into going to Sally's house because they had all planned a surprise party. As we made speeches, I thought about the time Sally and Marline took my son for the weekend so I could gain my strength. As I looked back, sending my three-month-old son away for the weekend was something I shouldn't have had to do.

To the rest of the staff at the York Town Health Center, Shereen, David, Nadine, Natilee, and Mr. Lewin, thank you for everything. Let me share a card I got from them the night before I left Jamaica. I read it over and over again to help me cope:

> When one door closes in our lives
> God always open another.
>
> When times are good, be happy, but when
> times are bad, consider God has made the
> one as well as the other.
> *Ecclesiastes 7:14*
>
> When we are facing disappointment in our lives
> Sometimes it's hard to see that this is also part
> of God's plan, but it's true.
> God knows what is best for us, and He will
> lead us to where we need to be.
>
> Have faith in Him and you will reach
> all the wondrous things that He has
> waiting for you.
> *D.L. McDaniel*
> *The card is a product of Blue Mountain Arts.*

These are the messages they wrote:

"I wish you all the best life has to offer. Take good care and I will always remember you. Luv, Sherine"

"Keep on smiling 'cause God is just going to keep on opening doors for you. I am going to miss you. Love, Nadine"

"I am going to miss u. My prayers will always be with u. Love 4 ever, Marline"

"I wish you the best God has to offer. As the card says, 'God knows best.' Love u always. Friends forever, Sally"

"Michelle, I am going to miss you. You are someone whom I always admire as having a very strong personality. I know you will achieve great things in life. Love always, Sonia"

"Don't be discouraged; don't you worry about a thing 'cause God has a plan for your life, you are clean, nice, loving, comforting, encouraging...And I consider myself blessed to have a friend like you, I appreciate all you have done. Someday you will find someone who appreciates you and your kids. Let your light continue to shine and remember that God loves you and He cares. He never gives you more than you can bear. In spite of whatever He gives, He is a problem solver and a burden bearer. So take everything to him in prayer. Love Natilee and family"

When my friend Sonia realized how bad my situation was, she said to me one day, "Michelle, Ian is not cheating on you because you're not beautiful or good enough. Look at Doreen Samuls. She is a former Miss Jamaica contestant and a popular radio announcer. She went through the same thing with her husband and look how beautiful and talented she is. So never think it is about you."

My girlfriend Stacey made a similar statement to me: "Michelle, look at Halle Berry. She is the woman that every man dreams of having. She is rich, famous, and very pretty, yet she has gone through two divorces. The men who got her still were not satisfied. Not even Princess Diana with all her beauty and royalty could escape it. It is not about you."

My undying gratitude goes to the following special people:

My friend Althea, who supplied me with books and tapes when she could not find enough words to say and who was there for me whenever I needed her. She brought me to the hospital when I went in to have my son, and we were there running up the stairs like teenagers, chatting and giggling as we went into the maternity section. After she checked me in, she gave me the *Woman Thou Art Loosed* Bible to read while I was in the hospital.

To my friends at the University of the West Indies: Heather, Janice, and Carlissa for your support.

To Mrs. Ford and her daughters for their support and understanding.

To Sonia for being there for me every step of the way and cheering me on.

To Jackie and Judith for being there for me over the years.

To Sheryl Morris, my high school teacher, who was always there for me and remained my best support whenever I was in need.

To Mrs. Ebanks for her understanding and support before, during, and after I left her son.

To my former supervisor at the Clarendon Health Department for her encouraging words as I left Jamaica.

To my cousin June for being there for me every step of the way, for believing in me and encouraging me.

To Shawna for her support.

To Tracy for taking care of my children and staying at my house way into the night.

To my aunt Avis for accommodating me.

To Basil, Danny, and Bunny, my cousins who supported me.

To Wayne and Crageton: Yes, I have seen grown men cry when they see my pain.

To my friend Lorna and her family for helping me and my children.

To my friends Jackie, Paulette, and their families, and especially Alicia for giving up her room to me and my children for a few months.

To Michelle for her love.

To the authors who have given me strength, power, confidence, hope, and inspiration during my broken dreams. To T.D. Jakes for *Woman Thou Art Loosed*, *Maximize the Moment*, and other books. To Harold S. Kushner for his books *When Bad Things Happen to Good People* and *The Lord Is My Shepherd*.

I sat across from the lady at the counseling center one day when I felt too stressed to go on. When I was finished telling her my story and the pain of my loses she pause for a while then said, you have achieved one thing so far, this lady must not be listening to me. I gave her a strange look then ask her what. She moved closer to me and softly said he is out of your life. She was right. She went on.

Starting over on a brand new path is very hard, but is much better than remaining in a relationship that is not nurturing to you as a woman. Look at you, you are a good person you gave him your best and you deserve a life of happiness and fulfillment that is exactly what I wish for you. We close the session but I will always remember those words, they were exactly what I needed .

If there is anyone I left out, I love you and thank you for touching my life and my children's lives. Now, all of you stand up and take a bow.

www.ingramcontent.com/pod-product-compliance
Lightning Source LLC
Chambersburg PA
CBHW020311290526
45784CB00003B/1473